WITH LOVE TO MY CHILDREN,

ATLANTA, ESTELLE, JAY,
KEIRA & AMBER BATES

Contents

Introduction	7
1. Have You Seen My Missing Penis?	11
2. The Miracle	17
3. When I Click My Fingers	21
4. I Want to See God Again	24
5. Where Are My Drugs?	27
6. Make Love – Not War	30
7. Total Recall	32
8. There's Nowt so Queer as Folk	36
9. Past Life Regression	51
10. Real People – Real Lives	67
11. The Rendlesham Forest UFO	85
12. Bizarre Therapy	93
13. Lady in Red	107
14. Hunt the Gunman	111
15. Buried Alive	115
16. A Royal Confession	124

Introduction

Alan Bates, successful author of *Hypnotic Star* and *Wide Awake*, is proud to present his latest book *Confessions of a Hypnotist*.

The most widely broadcast TV hypnotist in the world shares his hypnotic secrets that will captivate, entertain and enlighten you. *'Confessions'* is a comfortable, easy read that will provide thought provoking questions about our lives and give you an insight of just how powerful our minds really are. Proving Einstein's theory that we only use a small fraction of our mind and that with the right tools we can unlock the potential to obtain results that we have only dreamt about.

Read about the sexual pleasure of one lady that had multiple orgasms just on a click of her boyfriend's fingers, how an aging hippy was regressed back to Canada to meet God again, how a drug dealer got so high testing his cocaine that he forgot where he had hidden his illicit stash, and enjoy the emotional experience of the crippled young girl that walked again.

This book has been carefully crafted with true stories that will have your head shaking with disbelief, it will have you laughing out loud wherever you read it, proving the old cliché **'there's nowt so queer as folk'** as a most fitting introduction to this book.

IMPORTANT: all the stories in this book are true and so therefore all names, locations and indeed countries are changed to give total anonymity. If you are reading this book please rest assured that all hypnotherapy sessions are 100 per cent confidential and will never be discussed in public.

You now have an *overwhelming desire* to

        g e t   c o m f o r t a b l e

to sit back

      with a *nice cheeky glass of wine,*

forget the worries of the world

and join Alan

as **he** guides **you**

deep,

    d
      e
        e
          p

      ... into the psyche of the Human Being

FOR IT IS NOW TIME

TO

TURN

THE

PAGE!

1. Have You Seen My Missing Penis?

I love the buzz of the stage. There is something about the anticipation of a live audience, it gets into your blood. It's certainly in my blood, and I am sure that every stage entertainer, particularly the stand-up, the singer, the actor, the dancer, even the juggler and the musician, they will tell you the same. I have had several employment opportunities throughout my life but nothing can compare with the feelings one gets on stage. In saying that, I do receive an equal satisfaction from helping clients with psychological issues, although the similarly powerful emotions are on a different level.

I never relied solely on entertainment agencies for show bookings. In the earlier days of performing around university and college student unions, social clubs and, believe it or not, HRH prison officer's social clubs, I used to actively promote myself. In today's climate, lots of social clubs like those of the British Legion are folding due to falling attendance, but in their day they were packed to capacity, especially when an act was performing, and always at weekends.

The next story I offer is one I often tell, and always when performing in a theatre that requires an interval break.

In November 1997 I was contracted by the social secretary of an HRH prison service officer's social club in Kent, England. Kent is at least a four hour drive from Liverpool, close to where I am based, so by the time I reached my destination I was ready for a break. The welcoming committee was great and I was treated to a nice meal and non-alcoholic refreshments. By the time I had finished dinner and sound checked the venue I was ready to start the show. The club had picked up nicely and it was almost a full house. The audience consisted of mainly the prison service officers and administration staff, both males and females, along with their partners and friends. There were also some officers, still in uniform, who had just finished their duty shift and joined the social gathering for a few drinks.

I started my performance and was welcomed warmly by the audience who were eagerly anticipating a good show. It wasn't long before I had hypnotised my chosen few – six willing and excited participants. This particular show was of a two hour duration with a fifteen minute interval, the same format that I use whenever performing in the theatre. The first half of the show was going well and when it was time to take the customary theatre-style interval, to keep the audience entertained I set a task for all of the hypnotised volunteers to do during the break.

The first suggestion I gave was to a middle-aged lady; she was Little Bo Peep and had lost her sheep, and whenever she heard '*baa*' from the audience she would change her behaviour. This was the trigger that I placed in her subconscious mind, at which point she was to dash about trying to round them all up like Lassie at a sheepdog trial.

The next suggestion was to an older male. I gave him the task of being Santa Claus's little helper, 'the list elf', and that his duty was to go around the audience during the interval and ask everyone what they wanted for Christmas. I informed the audience that maybe their requests should not be boring, nor materialistic – and, also, that they could write a colleague's name instead of their own. I'm sure you can imagine the freedom such a setup affords, inviting all manner of risqué gift requests. This made the whole thing all the funnier as the lists and all the names were then read out in the second half of the performance.

On to hypnotised volunteer number three, who I shall name Paul. When Paul had joined the show at the very start he had displayed a negative attitude toward hypnosis, and so it made it even more meaningful – and funnier – that he was very susceptible to the process and that *he* was now one of the stars up there on stage. I suggested to him that his duty was to walk around the club and, upon encountering anybody drinking alcohol – virtually the whole audience, of course – he was to dole out a lecture on the demon drink, including a warning on the increased possibility one might end the night in bed with an unattractive person.

Suggestion number four was given to a younger male who was to walk around the tables where he would find that the contents of all the ashtrays was money – his money – and he needed to retrieve it all and keep it safe. He did this right away, and with gusto.

This was before the days of the smoking ban in public places, which came into force in England in July 2007. It is interesting to note that before the smoking ban these types of social clubs were full of smokers and the blue haze that filled the room could be clearly seen, particularly when the light passed through at a certain angle. Today's doctors would consider the non-smokers of those days to be as potentially 'at risk' as the smokers themselves, simply by breathing in this fug of secondary smoke.

As an Englishman, I am personally amazed and disappointed that my proud, educated and civilised nation was one of the last to implement the smoking ban.

The next suggestion I gave to another young man. He was at Hollywood's 'Oscars' awards ceremony, and his fellow audience members were in fact superstar actors. He would become incredibly excited, speak to as many stars as he could and get them to sign autographs on his arms.

The final suggestion leads me to the highlight of this story and Peter. Peter was an officer who had just finished his shift, still in prison uniform, who had decided out of pure curiosity to pop in for a pint and to see what this 'hypnosis thingy' was all about. And this curiosity had got the better of him at the beginning of the show when he joined in with the rest of the audience, locking his hands together to then find, to his dismay, that try as he might, he could not get them unlocked.

Lo and behold, Peter became the star of all stars that night. I suggested to Peter that his 'wedding tackle' had dropped off and that he dared not go home without it as his wife would possibly kick up a great fuss. His duty during the interval was to go around the club, discreetly, and ask random people if they had they seen his missing 'sausage'.

So with a click of my fingers we entered the interval, accompanied by a musical crescendo, and the seated audience were treated to a spectacular array of crazy antics. During this part of the performance, even in the very early days, we would observe the volunteers for their well-being. People all around the club were impersonating sheep with folk 'baa-ing' and whistling and shouting 'Come by', to the annoyance of a mithered little Bo Peep trying to 'pen' them in behind the seats. A steady line of people were queuing to give Santa's helper a Christmas wish list, but there was no sign of Peter and his missing 'todger'.

Where on earth was he? We looked everywhere; under the seats, in case he thought it had just fallen off there somehow, and in the toilets, in case he felt he may have flushed it away. But he was nowhere to be seen.

The fifteen minutes of interval expired and it was time to restart the show. I was introduced back to the stage and started the second part of the act by interviewing all the participants about what had happened during the break. The show was going exactly to textbook perfection and I couldn't have asked for a more responsive audience, but there in the back of my mind I had a niggling thought: where was Peter and his missing 'jolly roger'?

I was about ten minutes into the second half of the show when I happened to catch sight of a gentleman at the back of the club who was waving frantically to get my attention. Standing alongside the waving man was a worried Peter, and he was not alone. Behind poor 'pecker-less' Pete was a very large uniformed policeman with a big grin on his face. I welcomed Peter back and onto the stage to a thunderous round of applause. When I asked him live on stage where he had been, he replied forlornly, 'To the police station,' where he had asked the duty sergeant if anybody had handed in to lost property his missing 'tool'?

Luckily, the discerning desk sergeant, instead of applying a straightjacket immediately, kindly asked him where he had just come from, as he was still in his prison officer uniform, similar to a police uniform. Peter explained that he had finished his shift and attended the prison social club for a quick drink on his way home and the last thing he remembered was . . . locking his hands together at the Alan Bates Hypnosis show.

'I can see it all now,' said the duty sergeant, who by now had pieced together the puzzle of this missing 'Mr Wriggly' with good old-fashioned police detective work.

So, the lesson learned that day was to always include the suggestion that the hypnotised entertainers on stage will *not* leave the venue during the interval, and if there was an emergency, or any form of alarm, they were to come out of the hypnotic trance immediately and leave the premises.

Just to finish off here, and as repayment for all the fun we had had, I suggested to Peter as I brought him out of his trance state, that once he had found his missing penis it was going to be three inches bigger than before he lost it. And as this suggestion slowly sank in you should have seen the smile of contentment spread across his beaming face.

You now have the overwhelming desire to turn the page ...

2. The Miracle

As in every trade, and indeed every walk of life, learning the ropes is essential for development, and trial and error is all part and parcel of developing the skills required for a successful hypnotist to best deliver the end result. Whether it is to command a large audience on stage or to help a single client who suffers a debilitating illness or handicap, the end result is all important. The next story I tell taught me a valuable lesson in my early days as a developing stage hypnotist.

Circa 1981, I was booked by my agent, at the time based in the North East of England, to perform at a sports and social club in Lancashire. The occasion was to celebrate the 18th birthday of a young lady named Sarah. It was an afternoon performance and I arrived with my stage manager 'Blakey' to a very noisy audience with lots of excited children running around and bumping into us as we carried the heavy PA sound system into the venue. Once we had set up and sound checked we were all ready to start the show at our contracted time of 3.00p.m.

Observing the audience it was evident that everybody had their own agenda, chatting to friends and family, and I thought it was going to be difficult to command the attention of this preoccupied crowd. Just before I was due on stage I was introduced to Sarah by her parents, and I was a little shocked. Sarah was a very pretty girl but due to an unfortunate accident was disabled and confined to a wheelchair. She was really excited about my show and eagerly waiting for me to start, so without further ado I wished her a happy birthday and went to my dressing room to change.

Lights set, audience ready, it was show time! My introduction and music resonated throughout the building and I was pleased to be welcomed on stage by a very eager and enthusiastic audience. After a welcoming speech I requested the audience to sing Happy Birthday to Sarah at the top of their voices and then it was time to commence the show. Even at this very early time in my career I had an abundance of confidence and people skills, but nothing could have prepared me for what was about to unfold. During my initial hypnotic induction I used the hand locking technique to find the most susceptible subjects and, to my surprise, though wheelchair-bound, Sarah followed the instructions to a T and was highly susceptible, her hands truly locked together. She really wanted to take part in the show.

As it was her birthday, I was duty bound to give Sarah the best experience I could, but I had to adjust my routines to accommodate her disability. One of my routines at the time involved asking the participants what they wished for, granting their wishes under hypnosis, then letting them live the dream. When it was Sarah's turn she looked deeply into my eyes and said loudly into my microphone, 'I wish I could walk again!' I felt the whole audience's deeply penetrating eyes burrowing into me. The children up to this point had all been particularly noisy and lively, but now suddenly the whole room had become deathly silent. Without really considering, and without going into the consequences of my actions, I placed Sarah into a very deep hypnotic trance, which she took to very well, and then suggested to her subconscious mind that she could now overcome all of her fears, and that she could walk again naturally and unaided.

The deathly silence continued throughout all of these suggestions, right up until I clicked my fingers and Sarah's eyes opened wide. I offered my arm as a support and, after what seemed like ages to me, but which was in real time only a few seconds, she lifted herself out of the wheelchair. To the complete amazement of the audience, and myself, she proceeded to take a step forward. She wobbled and was understandably very unsteady, but I was there for her in case of a fall.

Slowly, she took a second step, then a third. By now the whole audience were giving their one hundred per cent attention, amazed at what had materialised, and I heard several voices exclaim, 'This is a miracle'. And that was what it felt like as it unveiled before our very eyes.

Sarah had not walked since her accident and now, at the celebration of her 18th birthday, she had walked the entire width of the dance floor. Blakey moved her wheelchair to receive her on the other side. Once she reached this point, she sat down and cried her eyes out with tears of joy, accompanied by her parents, family and lots of loving friends in the audience. I must admit that I did, too. It was such a moving moment. I was emotional but, rightly or wrongly, I also felt an all-powerful feeling coming over me. And this would need examining.

It was only when driving home after the show, when the feeling of power had subsided, that I analysed what I had actually done. I had not only taken a risk with the routine backfiring but, more importantly, I took a risk with the physical health of my volunteer, Sarah. Who knows what damage could have happened by applying pressure on muscles, joints and bones that had been paralysed and unused for such a long time, and beyond that also the psychological damage that could have occurred. I don't know what became of Sarah but I would like to believe I gave her the confidence to try to walk again and to gain from the confidence this may have given her. And witnessing what I had, and the effect it had, also gave me the confidence to believe in myself and to move towards, and then into, what would later become a major and important part of my future work – hypnotherapy.

It was this development with Sarah that started my realisation of what hypnosis could do for folk, and the depth and range of the mind. I was to have a similarly powerful experience happen again overseas many years later while working with a middle-aged lady who had damaged her foot. The hospital medical tests had proved conclusively that the physical damage had repaired itself but what the client lacked was the confidence in herself to walk again. And, sadly, there are no prescriptions for confidence. After three sessions of therapy she walked again unaided.

3. When I Click My Fingers

A hypnotist practising therapy can never be totally prepared for the outrageous reasons for which clients book appointments. But when the appointment details are taken and the purpose described as 'personal reasons', then one can logically presume that in the majority of cases it has to do with sex or is of a sexual nature.

This next case involves a person that I knew reasonably well, who I will call Alex. Alex was a good looking professional person that lived life to the full. He had several girlfriends and I think that each girl he was sleeping with deep down knew they were not the only lover or sexual partner in his life, but they seemed to be happy and content in his company. Alex contacted me one day with the complete consent of one of his girlfriends, that I shall name Helen, to book a session for sexual therapy. I suggested that rather than talk about it over the telephone with only Alex, it would be much better, fairer – and quicker in the long run – if we discussed it confidentially with both attending my office. We agreed on a date and time and I thought no more about it until the appointment day.

When Alex and Helen attended their appointment – knowing Alex as I did – I made sure I kept my professional head on throughout the hour, without allowing the conversation to roll as it usually does with friends. So, after the pleasantries, it was quite quickly down to business.

'What can I help you with?' I asked.

They looked at each other and Alex said that, by 'mutual agreement', Helen wanted me to hypnotise her so that during their lovemaking each time Alex clicked his fingers she would have an orgasm!

I was astonished by this request and had to think for a moment about it and all its ramifications. I told them clearly that this was a first for me, but as it was a mutual agreement, between two consenting adults, why not? Helen had clearly stated the desire to experience multiple orgasms during sex. So who was I to deny the request?

After giving them both a comprehensive talk about how hypnosis works, a simple psychological lecture and a 'Q&A' it was time to start the hypnosis. Helen was a good subject and within minutes she was showing the classic signs of entering a deep hypnotic state, REM (rapid eye movement), head rolling to one side and muscle relaxation. Helen was now in a profound state of hypnosis.

Before the session had started we had all discussed the method and outcome of her hypnosis, so I was now prepared to give her the psychological suggestion to enable her to sexually climax with the clicking of Alex's fingers alone. This was the trigger implanted deep in her mind, but it was only to happen when they were in bed making love and not for example while they were shopping in a supermarket, which might be embarrassing, or in any other public place for instance, nor for example if someone snapped their fingers for a waiter.

Intimate detailed suggestions were carefully crafted and embedded deep into the fabric of Helen's subconscious mind and, judging by the depth of trance state that she entered, I was convinced they were going to have lots of fun and games together.

Session over, I asked Alex to report back to me at some point to update me with the results and how things had worked out. Several days later Alex did indeed contact me, he was very excited on the phone and told me what had happened. Not only did it work, and even better than he had anticipated, but there was a twist to the story.

Helen worked for a local government department and held a senior position. After the first bedroom encounter, Helen had gone into work the following morning looking like she had been dragged through a hedge backwards. She had confided with her secretary and told her of the intimacy that she had experienced the previous night. When Alex called her office that lunchtime, her cheeky secretary asked if he could sometime click his fingers for her!

4. I Want to See God Again

I try not to look or sound shocked or surprised by people's requests regarding hypnotherapy. They may have struggled with their problem for years and may have suffered all kinds of shame and/or abuse.

In 2014, my manager contacted me regarding an individual case. Normally the appointment would have been taken, confirmed and rubber stamped for my attention in due course, but due to the intriguing nature of the therapy request she thought it better to run things by me first.

The client, that I will name Jonathon, was one of those aging hippies who had led a hedonistic lifestyle during the sixties and early seventies. During this period he had travelled to Canada to experience its natural beauty and great outdoors. His appearance was still reminiscent of the days of the permissive society, free love and flower power. His basic lifestyle at the time existed of regularly using mind-bending drugs, such as LSD and ayahuasca (the latter containing DMT (dimethyltryptamine), commonly known nowadays as the 'spirit molecule'. A number of indigenous peoples' shamanic traditions and religions use substances such as ayahuasca that contain DMT or similarly acting agents. This has led some people to consider DMT and the like as being more 'spiritual', safe and natural, rather than solely a powerful chemical hallucinogen.

During one of his mind-bending trips he was convinced that he was guided by spirit to a meeting with God. He explained to me that the feeling was overwhelming and incredible, not only the psychedelic colours and hallucinogenic atmospherics that are common with tripping, but, beyond all this, the purity of his experience was, 'Completely out of this world!'

It was so intense that he was near to tears as he described the emotions he had felt. Bearing in mind that Jonathon was a frequent tripper and knew the kinds of effects that mind altering drugs were capable of producing, this one experience, this trip or epiphany, whichever way you think of it, had deeply affected him and, forty eight years later, he wanted to go back. He wanted to meet God again, and he wanted me to take him back!

Jonathon explained that this one particular experience was very different to anything he had experienced before and that the entity which had guided him had taken him to the throne of God himself. God had then communicated with him telepathically and the feeling of love that emanated was all powerful. He wanted to experience this just one more time. He had tried several times in the past using various forms of drugs to reach that intense level again but was always unsuccessful, and now he was free from all drug taking.

After my standard psychological lecture and the hypnosis 'Q&A' we were ready to start. As I explained to him then, as I do to all my clients before any session, 'There is no guarantee that hypnosis will work. Hypnosis is not a magic wand.' But I was hoping as I said it, as I do with all of my clients, that it would work. And, as I hope this book shows, it often works even better than a magic wand.

Jonathon managed to reach a level of hypnosis that I was comfortable to work with, so I regressed him back to Canada, back to the time and place, and back to his state of mind of forty-eight years earlier. The human mind has the ability to suppress thoughts and emotions, but using regression therapy a competent hypnotist can guide a subject deep into the subconscious mind, back through the veils of time, to reconnect with the level of experience that meant so much to them.

I regressed him right to the very sacred place he needed to be. Once there, I gave him the psychological tools he required to continue the journey on his own, to guide or be guided, back to that inner space and time. And I waited quietly.

He had made me really feel the importance to him of his 'meeting with God' and I genuinely liked this man and wanted to help make his quest successful, although I had never done anything like it before. After a period of approximately fifteen minutes, I suggested he leave the regressed time and place and return to the present, local, everyday, real time. Slowly, I awoke his conscious mind and his eyes opened.

Postscript

Jonathon managed successfully to reach the time and the place of his initial experience, and he did indeed experience that same pure state of mind, but he was unsuccessful in meeting God again. It was a very intense, beautiful feeling, and one that was induced naturally this time, without mind modifying drugs. He was sad and disappointed that he did not get where he wanted to be, but he had enjoyed the natural feeling and thanked me sincerely for my effort.

5. Where Are My Drugs?

We all from time to time suffer forgetfulness. It's perfectly normal and, generally, if you have misplaced or lost a particular item, it usually turns up in the least expected place. The subconscious mind is continually processing vast amounts of data from the moment we are born and throughout our lives, only resting when we ourselves are finally laid to rest.

I like to think that we do not forget anything we experience in this life, that everything that we see, hear, taste or smell – however fleetingly or quickly, or largely unnoticed at the time – is still there, deep within us. It still resonates there, and that means that with the proper help and skilful guidance we can again re-see, re-feel, even re–live these buried events. Now, some memories are definitely not worth revisiting, but it has to be said that many would be really valuable to us, and very moving.

So, by using regression therapy it is possible to go back in time, and I am now going to give you an example. Think of something that is significant in your life, it may be meeting your partner for the first time, starting school, a new job, your first car; stop and think now. You have just done this and it took maybe seconds to do. So therefore you are in fact a time traveller, even though it was only inside your own memory. And if that memory is *very* real, and I am requested to guide you to make it *intensely* real, then you have actually travelled back in time to that scene.

For example, what if I was to hypnotise you and take you back in time to, say, your first day at school and, in slow motion, release memories of things that happened such a long time ago, for you to relive the senses, the smells, and the emotions, nervousness, joys and rapture of memories that have all been buried and forgotten such a long, long time ago, or that are hazy, faint and faded shadows of important times and people. During the hypnotic process it is possible to recall such events that have taken place in your life and are still stored dormant in the subconscious mind, rather like pictures or documents that remain vivid and vibrant in lost files on the hard drive of your inner computer. The event that I am going to describe next certainly startled me and I was really stuck for words!

In the summer months of June 2013, I greeted and welcomed a gentleman into my office. He was of stocky build, unshaven and rather agitated. I sensed something was not quite right but I could not work it out at first. The advanced paper work for the consultation stated that the client hoped I would be able to help him find a valuable lost item.

First impressions are always important, especially in my line of work, and you never get a second chance for a first impression, so getting it right psychologically is very important to me. I sat him in the therapy chair and asked him how I could help. His frankness took the wind right out of my sails.

'Look, Mr Bates, I will cut out the unnecessary small talk. I am a drug dealer and I have recently tested and bought a very, very large quantity of very potent cocaine, and, obviously, I had to try it. Afterwards, I was so high that I hid the drugs very well. So damn well that now I cannot find them!'

I sat looking at him with my mouth wide open for what seemed like ages. I had to explain to him, with a quivering voice – and, diplomatically, as he was a very big bloke – that unfortunately I would not be able to help him find his drugs.

He stood up, glared at me and stormed out of my office, without even paying for the consultation time. And not even a goodbye!

6. Make Love – Not War

Sex is a beautiful and natural part of being human. However, it is often considered a taboo subject to discuss and can lead to embarrassment, which is itself, of course, also a human emotion, a psychological feeling. Certain people find it very difficult, if not impossible, to manage.

All the stories in this book are true, but the golden rule with hypnotherapy must be that client confidentiality prevails – always and at all times. It is never my intention to embarrass anybody, so names are changed to protect the identities of the people involved, and as I practise in several countries, even if I have treated you, the reader, please rest assured that any story you find here is almost certainly not about you as in many cases I have treated similar clients, with equal responses, in several different geographical locations.

Listening to clients' problems, particularly with their sex lives, to me is not usually a shock or surprise – I have heard it all before, or, at least, most of it. The next story I have already covered in my last book, my autobiography *Wide Awake*. Five years ago, I had a pleasant middle-aged couple come to visit me. Their problem was that the wife would get drunk each and every night and beat the living daylights out of her husband, and then not remember anything the next day.

They still loved each other dearly but badly needed this alcoholic nightmare to go away and disappear – for good. In most of these types of cases I would usually, under hypnosis, ease down gradually the quantity of alcohol that was being consumed, over a period of time and with several sessions. This is to deal with it gently and to avoid harsh withdrawal symptoms, the 'cold turkey' effect of severe and sudden withdrawal from any addiction. After explaining this to my clients, I was asked by them, politely but sincerely, to forget this procedure in this instance as, if the treatment was successful, she was prepared to face the demons. Under the circumstances, and after a further explanation and discussion, I agreed to continue in the manner that the three of us had mutually agreed upon.

Two months later, they revisited me and bounced into my office holding hands, with big smiles on their faces. I was delighted to hear that the therapy had worked 100 per cent, but when I asked if there was anything else that I could help them with, the lady's head dropped and all eye contact was lost.

I knew immediately what it was but I gently waited as they gathered the confidence to explain. The husband took control over the conversation and said, 'Since the alcohol problem is now controlled, she has completely lost all of her sex drive.' Knowing she was very susceptible to hypnosis we pursued a further cure for this new problem and, after another deep session, I now hope and expect that the couple are having a blissfully happy and loving sexual relationship.

7. Total Recall

The human mind, *our minds* – the one that is reading this and the other that is writing – is hugely complex, and even though eminent neuroscientists, surgeons and psychiatrists the world over think they know how it works, I am really dubious. They are perhaps dealing with the approximately 1.4 kg (3 pounds) of stuff we have between our ears, and all its wiring and signals. I can't believe that that is the whole story. It just doesn't seem to go anywhere near far enough.

I believe we are not even touching the surface. We don't see signals, we see colours and recognise people. And the wiring cannot begin to allow for opinions or changes of opinion, never mind the input of feelings and emotion. In my view, we are nowhere nearer to discovering the tools to unlock its secrets. I know there are many people that feel this way, and a growing number of committed scientists are also thinking along these lines and researching different versions of how this thing called a brain works, as well as what 'mind' means in relation to that. Included in this are the very important questions that are still largely unanswered, such as, who are we? What is this consciousness of ours that seems to be completely unnecessary and yet so precious, which gives everything, including science, art, music, memories and even life itself, its value and meaning?

Psychology has come a long way in the last one hundred years, but we are still only in its infancy. However, I do believe that in time we will have a much greater insight into this fascinating subject.

During the late nineties, I performed at a private party in Wallasey, England, close to where I was born and brought up, and a friend of mine, Paul, volunteered to take part. I did my usual induction to endeavour to find a few susceptible subjects and was successful in getting three people, including Paul, to take part. As it was a relaxed, private affair, and not a public theatrical show, a lot of these people were known to me, and, more importantly, I was well known to them. I felt, therefore, that they would understand the spirit in which I approached the subject, and more importantly, of course, how I would work with the subjects, the people being hypnotised.

This meant I had the opportunity to play with the format much more and also had more time to experiment with very deep elements of hypnosis that I would not normally have the opportunity to use. I started with a simple suggestion to Paul where I made myself totally invisible to his eyes only.

During the induction, I had noticed that Paul had the ability to travel exceptionally deep, much deeper in fact than most hypnotised subjects that I usually worked with. So, at this point, Paul's brain/mind had now blocked all visual aspects of my physical body and he was reacting and communicating with me only via his sense of hearing. I then proceeded to wave my hands in front of his face. As his brain had blocked my physical presence, his eyes did not blink as they normally would have done – an automatic response of which we have no control, intended to protect our sensitive eyes from objects potentially on a collision course. At this point, Paul's eyes and brain were presumably seeing me, but not reacting. His eyes were open, light was going into them – but his mind, 'he', was not seeing me.

I then went one step further by jabbing my two fingers at his eyeballs, stopping just a few centimetres away from his pupils, and yet still no motor response from his eyelids. This is very impressive to witness. Maybe try this on your un-hypnotised friends and perhaps even risk making a bet with them, as it's impossible to keep your eyes static and open while in a conscious state of mind.

The next experiment I conducted has stayed in my memory ever since. I obtained a long, thin piece of paper, approximately one metre in length and seven centimetres wide; in fact, a receipt till roll. With a black heavy marker pen, I wrote at random along the paper from start to finish different numbers, symbols and characters. At this stage, Paul, with his eyes closed, was resting, but still under deep hypnosis. When I had completed all the symbols I could cram on the paper, I suggested to him that on the command of 'Wide awake!' he would open his eyes and scan the paper from left to right, and then from right to left, and memorise the content I had written on it from beginning to end. This process took him literally only four seconds to do. I then proceeded to turn toward my now eagerly enthusiastic audience, who were by now completely engrossed by the experiments.

Out of sight of the paper, I asked Paul to recite the contents from his memory, as written from left to right. As he did so, I exhibited the paper roll to the audience, step by step, as Paul coolly and calmly read out every number, symbol and character 100 per cent correctly. The audience, myself included, gasped at this achievement of **TOTAL RECALL!**

But it did not stop there. I next asked Paul to read aloud the roll from right to left. Without any hesitation nor any apparent struggle he read out in reverse order the first half of the content of the scroll before he started to get confused. If anything, this underlines the extreme difficulty of what he was in fact, for a time, doing so easily. Most of us know our alphabet very well, and we have used it all our lives, but very few of us could say it backwards without it written in front of us. The audience responded very well to this and gave Paul and the experiments a roof lifting round of applause.

    Just take a moment now to think how amazing this would be, if only we could utilise this capability in our daily lives, and if we think of expanding it out to all the different fields of life, imagine what we might achieve. Such is the inherent power we all have locked deep in our subconscious minds. Einstein said in 1920 that the conscious mind was only the tip of the iceberg, the subconscious was indeed the rest of it, proving yet again his theory that we only actually use a small fraction of our minds. With the correct tools, we can unlock and expand our potential abilities, to enable us to be happier and more successful in life and obtain results that in the past we have only dreamt about.

8. There's Nowt so Queer as Folk

Pussy Galore

Let me now take you to the stage of the once famous, or rather 'infamous', Henri Africa's show bar in Oldham, Lancashire, in the north of England. The mid-nineties was a rampant time for cabaret entertainment and my comedy stage show was frequently solidly booked. My good friend of many years, Paul Edwards, was the general manager of this venue and he managed to promote the show successfully and achieve a full house attendance.

Henri Africa's was a unique concept, a 'way-out' place where the motto seemed to be 'anything goes'. Transvestites worked the bar and stage areas and outrageous comedy acts were in abundance, ensuring the customers received a great fun night out. It was also, as you can imagine, a magnet for stag and hen parties, and many famous names appeared at this venue. But, sadly, as the saying goes, nothing lasts forever, and the club is no longer standing.

I waited backstage for my call time, clocking up the miles pacing backwards and forwards, just as many entertainers do and have done for many years in theatres and venues the world over, in eager anticipation and focused preparation for their curtain call. When I was given my five minute call it seemed to last an eternity, not helped by the adrenaline circulating around my brain at rocket speed.

I made my entrance to a very rowdy and excited audience that made me feel very welcome. Now it was my turn to please them. Following a few jokes and a basic introduction to hypnosis, and after applying my hand clasp susceptibility induction, I managed to get fourteen willing subjects on stage.

Usually I would get the twelve or fourteen subjects in a row at the front of the stage, directly in front of the audience – they are the stars after all. But, due to the small size of the stage, I had to position two rows of seven chairs with a walking space between the rows. On the front row there was a very pretty blonde girl dressed 'attractively' – as I later learned, very scantily – and the men in the club were jockeying to get nearer to the stage and were whooping with merriment.

At this point it dawned on me that the audience, certainly the first few rows, were privy to something that I simply wasn't seeing. Due to the raised stage, and virtue of the fact that all my show volunteers and I were rather compacted on it, I had completely failed to see that the pretty young blonde girl was not wearing any underwear! I was probably the only one in the theatre who was still unaware of this fact – certainly it sounded that way. Complemented by a very, very short dress, and sitting with her legs 'defiantly placed', she gave every young man, and probably some of the older men, too, a racing pulse, as you can imagine.

I had to do something as the situation required immediate action, so I stood in between the audience and the blonde, which I must say felt a bit like standing between a lion and his lunch. I then asked her, very politely, if she would mind me removing the trance state and allowing her to return back to the audience to watch the show. As you can imagine, of course, this led to massive booing and jeering from the crowd, but her reply was surprising and took the wind right out of my sails.

'No, thank you very much, Mr Bates. I want to take part in the show and that's the reason I have paid to come here tonight.'

The crowd loved this, of course, and I was now in a bit of a dilemma as I needed to sort the problem out as respectably and as quickly as I could. I had to think rapidly and, to make matters worse, all my communication was live on the microphone, so the audience were aware of what I was saying. Thank goodness they couldn't hear what I was thinking!

The first tack I tried was to make a joke, saying that, maybe, when she had been getting ready to come to the show that she had perhaps forgotten to wear something? She just looked at me quite blankly.

'Something small, perhaps, but very, very important?' I said to the deafening silence of the audience.

'No,' she replied brazenly. I could hear all the air being sucked out of the room.

'But you have no knickers on!' I blurted out, which on reflection was probably not the ideal thing to say. But I can assure you, dear reader, that it was what absolutely everyone was thinking. I heard it echo throughout the whole room for only a second, and then all hell broke loose.

The audience went into a frenzy, even the girls in the audience were astonished. The air was thick with all manner of buzz and commentary, which I knew I had to step into, somehow, to take control of the direction we were heading in.

And then she silenced them again. 'In fact, I dressed particularly carefully tonight. Trust me, Mr Bates, I deliberately came out dressed this way.'

I had to change something fast, very fast, here. There was no way I could allow the show to career along in this manner. It had finally dawned on me that she was very aware of exactly what she was doing and was distinctly enjoying the fact she had over two hundred pairs of eyes glued to her private parts, and yet she was not at all fazed. I felt she was even getting off on what I could only see as extreme attention.

I can assure you that it was not her personality that they were the slightest bit interested in. And, at that point, I distinctly felt that I had a responsibility here, to the audience, to the management, and also to this lady. I had no idea what was going on in her mind nor what might have put her in this state. She didn't look drunk as she was so calm and collected, but she may have been. She may even have taken some other substances, or perhaps all of these things. I'll never know but at that moment I had to make a decision.

I offered her a compromise. I asked very politely, if, for me, she would sit on the back row on the stage, more comfortably and neatly tucked away from the voyeurs, and if she could try to keep her legs closed as her skirt was very short. Thankfully, she accepted and I managed to pull the show off very well indeed. We even enjoyed a few wicked little innuendos about the naughty blonde beauty on the back row, which she took in good heart and well in her stride, so to speak.

American Dream

If you too are thinking to yourself how on earth a person can do such a thing as the lady in the previous story, well, the next story may really shock you.

Once again, in the nineties, I had a regular slot at a nightclub named Bentley's in North Wales, UK. I played the music and compered the cabaret shows that were billed every week, and the club was invariably very busy, which always feels good to any performer. I used to arrive early, before the doors opened to the public, preferring to do this as it helps things to run smoothly before 'curtain up'.

The first clients through the door one particular cold and bleak Welsh November evening were a couple from the United States. As they were early birds – it was 9.00 p.m. – I decided to join them for a drink. They initially struck me as a nice couple, early thirties, professional, pleasantly dressed, on business locally. We sat in the cocktail lounge and chatted away for about twenty minutes after which I wished them a pleasant evening and bid them goodbye, leaving to go to work.

At around midnight, with the club completely full, there was a sudden commotion within the audience, shouting and swearing. To my horror I watched as several burly security men literally dragged the American couple – that 'nice American couple' – away through the crowds in a very rough and rapid manner. The fire exit crashed open and the two of them were propelled from the club and out into the car park.

'What the hell has gone on there?' I thought. I was unsettled and the audience was, too. I really needed to find out what had just happened, particularly as to what might warrant those people I had chatted with so pleasantly earlier being thrown out in such a manner?

As soon as my slot had finished I met with the head of security. I knew him well. He ran a good club, a 'safe' place to enjoy yourself. I asked him what on earth had just happened?

'Alan, sit down,' he said and directed me to take a seat. 'You are never going to believe what I am about to tell you.' I could tell he was shocked and that surprised me. He'd been working clubs for years and he didn't shock easily, so by now I was almost on the edge of the chair with anticipation.

He shook his head as he spoke. 'Alan, listen, I thought I had seen it all, what with twenty years on the job and all.' He explained that the American couple had been drinking cocktails and champagne. The man had become rather intoxicated and had been trying to arrange a 'threesome', his eyebrows went up at that word, 'Between him, his girlfriend, and Alice, the pretty little cocktail waitress. This was all supposed to happen after the club closed, back at their hotel.'

We knew the waitress was not that type of kid. She was fairly young and intelligent and certainly didn't need this obnoxious level of abuse while she was trying to work. She had noticed the Yank masturbating at the bar. He had stood up off his barstool as she approached and ejaculated all over the bar, his girlfriend – and even in the ashtray. Alice whacked him over the head with a drinks tray, screamed and pressed the panic alarm button, all at the same time. The security came running from all directions and dragged him out with his trousers round his ankles.

'All's well' as they say. Alice was given a round of applause by her colleagues on the bar and a coffee break and the Americans disappeared off into the misty Welsh night. I hope he didn't get frostbite.

Little Devil

I experienced another strange situation at this same club just a couple of weeks after the above episode involving the crazy American couple, which really made me think there's **'Nowt so queer as folk'**.

What happened was that an unaccompanied, smartly dressed and attractive girl in her early twenties approached me and enquired why I was wearing a bandage on my arm. I had recently had a small tattoo removed and it was bandaged for protection. I explained the reason and she replied, 'Interesting, I have a tattoo as well, you know. Would you like to see it?'

I asked her where it was and her eyes looked downwards. 'Down there. Would you like to see it?'

Innocently, without a second thought, I replied that I would, though not really knowing what to expect. To my surprise, the stranger lifted up her dress, pulled her knickers to one side, and lo and behold she had a little red devil tattooed on her private parts! I was stuck for words, and she was really chuffed with my embarrassment. She smiled from ear to ear as she put her devil away, winked at me, rolled her dress down and walked off into the crowd.

What's in Your Knickers?

This next story reminds me of the humour and the sharp wit for which the folk of Liverpool are famous. While performing in a social club in Liverpool, I had performed my 'lottery' sketch, which involved the star of the show, a buxom blonde. Under hypnosis, the blonde had been informed that she had won the national UK lottery and had had a cheque presented to her to the value of one million pounds. After the photo session and the interview about what she was going to do with her new fortune – which is very funny for the audience, and particularly the friends or family they have with them – I requested her to conceal the cheque on her person in a safe place. Now, 99 per cent of women in my shows will automatically hide the cheque in their bras. Not our buxom blonde, though. It went straight down into her knickers. At this stage, I put her back to sleep and suggested that she would now completely forget about winning the lottery and the cheque.

At the end of the show, when she was the last participant on stage, I asked her, hypothetically, if she won the lottery, would she buy everybody in the club a drink. She replied, of course she would. I then asked her again, that if she had won the lottery and was in possession of a cheque for one million pounds, and the cheque was signed by me and made payable to her in her own handwriting, would she still buy everybody a drink? She again replied that she would.

At this point, my sound technician played a drum roll and I suggested that the very cheque we were talking about was located inside her knickers! She looked at me with a defiant stare and said, 'You can f*** right off, I don't know who put it there, I already have one c*** in my knickers and I certainly don't want another.' I was speechless!

Trouble at the Toilet

It is often said, and believed to be true, that it was always the men that misbehave on a night out after copious amounts of alcohol. However, while I don't completely disagree, as there is plenty of evidence that it does happen, with my own experience based on observation in this industry, the fairer sex can be equally, if not far more, outrageous.

I hope I have always conducted myself respectfully on stage. Cheeky? Yes, absolutely, but always knowing where to draw the boundary line. While performing in Dubai, I was told about the antics of a British hypnotist whom I know quite well – mentioning no names, of course – but he is known to go 'over the top' on occasions. Apparently, he was working at a five star hotel around the corner from my venue, and during the interval he had hypnotised a bloke to stand outside the men's toilets, saying to each man in a whisper as he entered, to the delight of the audience, 'Hey mate, do you fancy a w***?'! As much as this makes me laugh I could not do that sort of sketch.

Chelsea's Rapture

A lot of comedy stage hypnotists plagiarise other performers' routines. I have always tried to keep my routines and content different from other hypnotists and a lot of the material that I present on stage I have written myself. Even in the early days, I was never really an outrageous over-the-top performer. But I had a flashback recently that is worth a mention for the intensity of response I received from a show while working in Manchester, England.

The stage was set, my volunteers all eager and excited, and the audience were delighted that the manager of the venue, whom I shall call Chelsea, had volunteered herself onto the stage. Chelsea was a tall, attractive and single thirty-five year old, with long black hair.

Halfway through the show, I suggested to my hypnotised stars that I had a magical right hand, and if they were to shake it, the feeling would be sensational – orgasmic, in fact. Well, I am sure you can imagine now how funny this was! Bearing in mind it is all in the mind of the hypnotised person on how he or she interprets the suggestion.

The girls in the show were desperate to shake my hand, and, yes, even the boys, too, and the routine was working super well, until the audience exploded into serious fits of laughter. I turned my attention to the audience and followed their eyes to see what was giving them the serious giggles. To my shock, Chelsea was stretched out in the chair, jeans unzipped, her hand inside her jeans, pleasuring herself.

I immediately stopped her, woke her up and removed her from the stage. I think I was more embarrassed after the show than she was, even while I was enjoying a nice cup of tea with her. She laughed it off and said, 'Oh well, that will give the audience something to gossip about, won't it!'

Even while writing this book I had an embarrassing situation during a comedy show in Malta. I work a lot on this beautiful island where I am now a household name. On this occasion, I was presenting a Christmas comedy special during which I was unsure about the sex of one of my stars on stage. 'Is it a girl or is it a boy?' I kept asking myself. The person's name didn't help either. I made the decision that it was a 'she' and the show went without a hitch and was very well received. At the end, I thanked the stars on stage, shaking hands with the guys and giving the traditional Mediterranean kiss on both cheeks to the ladies, including my 'he/she'.

Billboard for Christmas comedy show, Malta

After the show, when I was book signing, the mother of the 'he/she' approached with a smile. 'Alan, do you know the sex of this person on stage?' she asked.

I stalled and thought on the spot. 'She's a girl,' I replied.

Mum laughed and said, 'Sorry, Alan, but that's my son!'

Police Sergeant Bob

My next tale along these lines is a story not directly associated to my work or hypnosis but was revealed to me whilst swapping stories over a pint of beer with a retired village policeman that I shall name Bob.

While I was a teenager growing up in the small town of Moreton, in the Wirral, England, there was an 'old school' village policeman named Bob. Bob did not suffer fools gladly and all the local youth were scared of him due to his no-nonsense attitude. Bob was well built and had a very large handlebar style moustache which distinguished him from any other police officer, and he also carried a truncheon. For example, if you were insubordinate, he would grab hold of you and give you a hard slap on the head and say, 'Go home and tell your parents that Bob has slapped you for being cheeky.' The kids did not dare to tell because if they did they would get another clip off their parents for being disrespectful, such was the respect that the kids had for their elders during the time that I was growing up.

Many years later, long after old Bob had retired, my father and I would have a beer or two with him at a local pub on a Sunday afternoon, and he told me a story that has stayed with me ever since. I have since retold this tale while socialising with several serving police officers around the world, including the chief of police in Malta and detectives in Singapore. They rolled over in laughter and vowed to pull the same trick given the opportunity.

Just like a lot of trainees in various other occupations, rookie cops have pranks pulled on them by the officers they are stationed with. One cloudy autumn night while on night shift duty, the new recruit was instructed by Bob to check the back of the local shops to make sure they were locked and secure. This was standard procedure and involved walking down a dark alley with a torch. But, unknown to the new bobby, Bob and another colleague had already visited the alleyway earlier and taped a drawing pin to the gate latch on one of the shops, then scooped up some dog poo on a stick and put it over the drawing pin. In Bob's mind, this was a sure way to check if the new boy was doing his job properly.

Moments later, the new constable rushed at the police car, angry as hell and shaking his hand. Bob locked the police car doors and was howling with laughter inside, as the poor recruit had done his job and checked the gate latch, but the pin had pierced his thumb and, with a natural reaction, he had put his thumb in his mouth!

Sadly, Sergeant Bob is now no longer with us, but this story will help keep his memory alive.

Madam Whiplash

An interesting part of my work is that I get to meet celebrities, famed for stage and screen, with whom I have often partied on nights out. In the early nineties, I was performing comedy at the King George's Hall theatre in Blackburn, England, and unknown to me several *Coronation Street* actors were in the audience. The immensely popular *Coronation Street* is the longest running weekly soap on British TV and amongst the guests that evening were Lynne Perrie ('Ivy Tilsley', her character's name in the show) and her friend, the famous 'Madam Whiplash', Cynthia Payne, a sex party 'hostess'.

Cynthia made the headlines in the seventies and eighties when she was acquitted of running a brothel. She first came to national attention in 1978 when police raided her home and found a sex party in progress. Men paid with luncheon vouchers to dress up in lingerie and be spanked by young women. Police found 53 men at her residence, in varying levels of undress, which included a peer of the realm, an MP, a number of solicitors, company directors and several vicars. A cartoon in the press at the time showed a vicar in bed with a prostitute, confronted by a policeman. 'I demand to see my solicitor,' said the vicar, 'who is in the next bedroom.' When the case came to trial in 1980, Cynthia was sentenced to eighteen months in prison, reduced on appeal to a fine and six months. She actually served four months in Holloway prison.

After the show, I was invited to a party in an old farmhouse near Manchester to celebrate the birthday of a member of the *Coronation Street* cast, and I gladly accepted. On arrival, I was presented with a glass of Châteauneuf-du-Pape and ushered to a minstrel's gallery to sing 'Fever' with 'Ivy'. I knew the words to the song but embarrassed myself terribly as singing is certainly not my forte.

The business card of 'Madam Cyn'

'Ivy', however, was really good. The guests were taking it in turns to do a party piece, so I decided to do what I know best – hypnosis. 'Ivy' offered herself up, and she was a good subject. I managed a fifteen minute display that enthralled the guests.

Cynthia tried but was unsuccessful. At the end of my demo she winked at me and gave me her business card, the famous 'sex luncheon voucher'!

My Life as a Sex God

Derek Acorah, the famous TV spirit medium, and I were performing our joint show 'The Paranormal Experience' one evening at a club in Liverpool when, during the interval, the dressing room door opened, and in walked a rather pretty brunette. Derek and I were startled as we were not expecting visitors and our visitor startled us even further when she asked me out loud, 'Can I have sex with you?'

The only other time I had such a direct request was while touring the Gulf States. I had been in Oman, on my own, sunbathing beside a beautiful hotel pool in the late afternoon sun, when a middle-aged lady, older than myself, whom I had never met before, swam right up to my sun lounger and gave me a 'Hi.'

I sat upright and responded with, 'Hello.'

The next words out of her mouth were, 'I am sorry to be so rude and straightforward, but will you have sex with me?'

I was again speechless, literally in this case, as I was desperately trying to think of an answer. 'No,' I replied.

Now I am sure the male readers are either thinking that this is the Sunday school version for the under-tens, or thinking 'What a silly sod!', but, really, I had a girlfriend at the time and it was the right thing to say. The cheeky lady then asked if I would buy her a beer instead.

Now, this seemed a much more civilised request, and I have to admit I was flattered and curious to find out which of my many wonderful qualities had got her engine revving. So I agreed to this request and over a cold beer we got chatting. I can't even remember her name but I do remember that she was from the United States and, if my memory serves me correct, she was a school teacher. As it turns out, it was not my irresistible vital charm that had pulled her across the swimming pool like a migrating salmon but the more down-to-earth reason that she was on her own and, as she openly admitted, was very lonely and didn't have many friends. She just wanted sex and some male company and thought I looked a suitable candidate.

Another celebrity I had the pleasure of working with was Peter Kay, the northern English comedian, in 2001. This was during the time that Peter's career was rocketing after his successful TV series *Phoenix Nights*, and I was looking forward to meeting and working with him. The show was in the Great Hall at Exeter University, England.

On arrival I was directed to the dressing room that I was to share with Peter, and when we were introduced I instantly took a liking to him. I have an ability to pick up on people, via my intuition, and the vibes I received were good ones. We chatted for a while and I noticed that Peter had a mark on his eye that resembled a black eye. I asked him if he had been involved in a fight, to which he replied, 'No, it's a birthmark!' I actually blushed and felt just a little foolish.

9. Past Life Regression

As well as using hypnosis in the traditional formats, that is stage comedy and hypnotherapy, I can also induce a trance state to allow people to travel back in time to a past life. This is a fascinating subject, one about which I could write a separate book and maybe one day I will. I believe it is worth giving you, the reader, insight into this subject. I have also covered past life regression in my last book, Wide Awake.

For several years, I performed alongside the famous TV spirit medium Derek Acorah, touring our theatre show, The Paranormal Experience, around the UK. I have many good memories of our work and friendship, Derek really opened my eyes to the esoteric world and I have shared just a sample with you below. So, without further ado, let me welcome you to 'past life regression' but first, an extraordinary story of an exorcism.

Exorcism

Derek often received calls from people who claimed they were being haunted, and we were often asked if we could help. We called it 'Ghost Busting', and every so often he would ring up and say, 'Alan, another ghost busting job has cropped up. Do you want to come?' I was always there in a flash. I was now mentally strong enough to handle paranormal activity. Gone were the times when I could not move around in my old haunted thatched cottage after dark. I witnessed Derek successfully exorcise several homes and business premises using a technique he had mastered over time to rid spirits – good and evil – from both places and times in which they didn't belong.

One particular exorcism has stayed in my mind. The mother of a sixteen-year-old boy from Liverpool contacted Derek claiming a spirit was wrecking her family, her young son near to having a nervous breakdown. In cases like this, it didn't matter how busy our schedules were, we dropped everything and went to their assistance. It was interesting how the story unfolded.

Upon arriving at the very pleasant, semi-detached family home near Liverpool, England, Derek immediately detected the presence of a spirit. We sat around a table in the lounge, drinking tea with the mother of the family, her two daughters and young son, who all looked pale and totally drained. None of them made a peep as the mother explained her story. For several weeks, her son claimed to have been woken up many times during the night by the duvet cover being dragged off him in bed.

The poor lad didn't understand what was happening, but it evolved into a more serious problem when one particular night, as the cover had been pulled down, he felt hands around his neck and started to choke. Just as he was about to pass out, the hands let go, and he screamed for help. His mother woke up and rushed into his room to find her son trembling and in a very distressed state. His younger sister had also witnessed this grim presence in his bedroom.

We asked the boy to take us alone up to his room, so we could have his version of events, and during his explanation he broke down and wept. Our hearts went out to him; he was a nice young man and clearly had a genuine problem. I then escorted him downstairs to sit with his mum and sisters, and re-joined Derek in the boy's bedroom. As soon as I went back in the room I could feel it. Derek had his eyes closed and, in silence, focused on the energy in the room. The temperature had dropped dramatically and I could really sense a strong presence. After several minutes, he said, 'Alan, I am now getting a clear picture of what has happened here. We must go downstairs and again talk to the family.'

Derek explained to all of us that the boy's father had witnessed a motorbike crash in the nearby country lanes and had rushed to the man's aid. The family nodded their heads in agreement. The motorcyclist had died in their father's arms and, upon returning home, the confused spirit had attached himself to their father and then resided in the family home. He explained that the spirit was not evil but had not passed over, and so was expressing his anger and confusion. This was being picked up by the young boy who was very sensitive and 'open'.

Then came the twist in the story. Derek astonished us all by saying he had contacted the boy's father, who had recently died of a heart attack, and passed on from him messages of love. The expressions on the family's faces were a picture; they had not mentioned anything about their father's recent passing, and certainly nothing about the motorcycle accident. Derek had once again proved his genuine 'gift'. He informed the family that we were next going to go back to the room where he would attempt to persuade the spirit to leave.

We set the room ready for the 'candle rite,' laid out the crystals and flowers, and Derek asked me to assist by focusing on peace and sending out thoughts for the spirit, while he made contact. After about twenty minutes of silence, the atmosphere in the room changed dramatically. It felt like a heavy burden had been removed from my shoulders and the room became serene and peaceful. He further explained that the spirit had not accepted the fact that he had died in the accident; he was confused and had become very frustrated because nobody would listen nor pay any attention to him. That was why he vented his anger on the boy, because he was open to the spirit world and could sense his presence.

During the candle rite, a departed female family member of the motorcyclist appeared before Derek and assured him and the spirit it was time for the cross-over, and the relative was there to guide him. The spirit departed, and we were both left emotionally drained. We went downstairs with the family for a final cup of hot tea and assured them that they would not have any more problems.

Each time we conducted an exorcism, it was a very rewarding experience. I would never have even believed I would witness one in all my life, never mind be involved in a small way.

With all my experience of past life regression, I have only made contact with two famous people. You may think that I would encounter lots of famous historical personalities, but this is certainly not the case. The first case was during a show that Derek and I were presenting at Fort Regent, in St. Helier, on 30 October 2010, on the beautiful island of Jersey, in the Channel Islands. One of the volunteers was regressed back in time to apparently being a well-known opera singer in Paris. Sadly, I do not have the information on this regression as a copy was not made when the recording was presented to the participant. The second case – 'regression two' – below, is of a more sinister nature, and the very subject is still drawing world fascination.

But first I would like to share some of my views on this very interesting subject, so, read on!

What Is Past Life Regression?

This is a question I frequently get asked and I usually answer by giving the following information. To my mind, we have four possible descriptions of what is happening.

1. Past life regression is a genuine psychic phenomenon, where contact is assisted by an induced hypnotic state that links to some historically lived experience, which may be documented and able to be checked and verified.

2. Past life regression is a manipulation of the imagination and fantasy, like a sort of controlled dream. As in a detailed and lucid experience of unconscious material, a story is weaved that is unrelated to any historic, and therefore real characters, who ever lived. Such information, of course, would be unverifiable, no matter how true they sounded.

3. Past life regression is a direct experience of genetically inherited information. For example, someone might perhaps be seeing vivid images from an *ancestor's* life – say, a great grandfather's memories of the First World War.

4. Past life regression is utter nonsense.

Throughout history, mankind has sought answers to the many mysteries of life. Since the dawn of time – and many years before Christianity – people have believed in life after physical death. But it has always been just that – a belief – and an act of faith, without any scientifically accepted proof. The sceptics, atheists, materialists – call them what you will – have always decried the evidence.

Many religious movements – Buddhist, Hindu, and some Greek philosophers – teach that reincarnation is the way that we, as human souls, develop merit. Our spirits pass from one incarnation on the earth plane to heaven / hell / nirvana, or whatever other name one may give to the appointed place for some form of judgement. Souls then achieve this state permanently, unless lacking in some way – or if the soul actually chooses to return – wherein the soul reincarnates back into the world.

In other words, we have our entrances and our exits, and one soul, in its time, must play many parts. We are, then, unconsciously, the sum of all those previous parts, yet within our individual psyche exists the memory of all our eternal life.

My method of unlocking the secrets of our past lives lies within the mystery of using the hypnotic trance to deepen people's ability to focus. The subjects are placed in a hypnotic state and then proceed to travel back in time to a past life. In this deeply relaxed state they can link to and relive the parts they played while incarnated in a different body, in a different time and place.

Many of us have experienced the near reality of a memory, indelibly imprinted on our minds, as we conjure up almost forgotten images from some important event in our lives. So it is with the regressed subjects - back they go, beyond the first memories of childhood, deeper and deeper they travel, passing the point of birth, conception and on into the mysteries of their previous life.

Witnessing a professional hypnotist working with a good subject may change your understanding of life as we comprehend it.

Regression One

On 22 March 2011, Derek and I were performing at the Garrick Playhouse Theatre, near Manchester, UK when I experienced one of the most amazing emotional regressions that I have ever witnessed. We were performing to a full house, the audience all eagerly waiting and ready to participate. Shortly after we had made our joint stage entrances and been introduced, Derek retired from the stage and I commenced my induction. Nothing could have prepared me for what we were about to tap into.

I had twenty willing participants on stage and nine of them were successfully regressed into past lives, all living in long forgotten times – and then I made contact in a past life with a lady named Joyce Ashton.

Joyce was deeply regressed to the Second World War and was living in Dewsbury, a small town near Leeds, UK with her husband, Thomas, and their young son, Robert. Thomas Ashton was a British soldier, an engineer, and held the rank of private. Thomas was killed in enemy action in Belgium on 2 October 1941, but his body was never recovered.

Meanwhile, Joyce was raising Robert single-handedly, contributing to the war effort by making tank shells in a munitions factory, named Steeton's. Steeton's, it seems, was a really big factory and people were bussed in from a twenty mile radius to work there. Lots of day-to-day information was recorded about her life in general, including St John's School and Anglican Church, which her son Robert attended. The feeling that I was receiving from Joyce was one of deep sadness, due to the loss of her husband. By now, the entire theatre audience were sitting on the edge of their seats, listening in complete silence, and you could have cut the atmosphere with a knife.

I then progressed with the timeline of this regression incarnation to Joyce's eventual passing. I guided her to the last moments of that life, and she relived it for us, sharp with tears and sadness. Joyce gave an accurate account of how she worked and how to pack down the explosive charge on a press. There was an accident – a shell exploded and killed four people, including Joyce. Joyce was working on the press with three other women when a spark ignited the gunpowder and blew the press to pieces, killing all of the women. When I asked what her last thoughts were, she replied with tears rolling down her cheeks: 'Who is going to look after my child now?' The audience gasped with emotion, such was the atmosphere in the theatre. After the regression had ended, I brought Joyce forward to the present time, and by now she was fully aware that some powerful emotion had moved her deeply due to the fact that her eye mascara and makeup, mixed with her tears, had run into her lap.

The regression subject was a lady named Gillian Perry, from Manchester. Gillian is a calm, intelligent and down-to-earth person, who has never been to Dewsbury and was unaware of the entire event.

Postscript

Research was conducted into the information that we had received during the regression and it transpired that Steeton's ammunition factory did exist, but sadly all that is left now is just a small square red brick building, named the pillbox, and, surprisingly, it is a 'listed building'. We could not find any records for this particular accident, but a lot of accidents were hushed up for morale and propaganda purposes and, at most, received an inch or two in the local paper, with no mention of exactly where the people died, other than 'a factory'.

St. John's School and Anglican Church, which her son Robert attended, exists in Dewsbury. There are registered births and deaths for Joyce and her husband, a birth entry for her son, but not a death certificate. Can you imagine the consequences if a search for her son was successful and what it would be like to re-unite them today? There is the possibility that he may still be alive. Maybe he was evacuated to Australia or Canada and adopted after the war – a lot of maybes, I know - but maybe his mother still needs to know he has had a good life. We may never know, but one thing is sure, Gillian had an amazing past life regression and a life-deepening experience.

The jewel in the crown in our research was the discovery of T. W. Ashton on the war memorial in Crow's Nest Park, Dewsbury.

Regression Two

On 7 September 2006, I was presenting a show at the Haydock Cricket Club in Lancashire, UK. This evening, the audience members were very excited. One could feel the atmosphere upon entering the auditorium and I was very keen to start the performance.

As usual I had twenty volunteers on stage and I was happy with my delivery and presentation, and, of course, the quality of the regressions, being most important. Halfway through the show, I regressed a middle-aged, well-spoken lady into a very deep trance state, and while communicating with her in a past life, it transpired she lived in London, and her name was Mary Kelly. The year was circa 1888 and her regressed incarnation was a working prostitute. All aspects of her private and working life unfolded on my stage, including Mary providing sexual services to seamen, and when I mentioned different nationalities, including the French, she remarked that she had once worked in a brothel in Paris. Mary also added that she had an illegitimate child. She said that times were very hard and she was leading a very sad life.

As the dialogue continued, and the information continued to flow, I guided her to the final part of her incarnation, and she started to tell me that she was brutally murdered. At this point, a man in the audience stood up and shouted loudly, 'Mary Kelly was the last prostitute to be murdered by Jack the Ripper!' I did not know this, but now the audience were buzzing with excitement. At the end of the session, once the regression subjects were returned to 'local time', I proceeded to interview this lady, live on stage. She had no memory of what had happened, to where she had travelled, nor to who she once had been. I was teasing her over the microphone, to the delight of the audience, when I said, 'Would you like to know what work you did in London in 1888? This rather reserved lady was curious as to why the whole audience and I were focusing on this particular point. She said, 'Yes. Please tell me.' And, after a little more teasing and coaxing of her curiosity, I said, 'You were a prostitute. And, it gets worse – you were murdered by Jack the Ripper!' The expression on her face was priceless. You could see she was genuinely taken aback, speechless. I used my charm and cheeky demeanour to best effect and reassured her that this was in the past and bore no reference on her present life.

Postscript

After the show, I was so excited to get home to research information on Mary Kelly. I was thrilled to bits as everything she said during the regression was very accurate. She also gave us additional information that is not in the public domain. Looking back, I believe I sadly missed the opportunity to ask her the most important question – the identity of Jack the Ripper. If I had done so, we may have had the identity and the answer to an age-old mystery.

Regression Three

In 2008, The Paranormal Experience tour was booked into the Gladstone theatre, near my former home in the lovely 'garden village' of Port Sunlight, Wirral, UK. The theatre sits beautifully within the *olde worlde* heritage village that was built by Lord Leverhulme, the founder of the world famous Sunlight Soap Empire. He built the village at the turn of the century for his workers as a deliberate attempt to create a village full of the valuable social amenities for a healthy and happy life, for all his workers. There are allotments, churches, a hospital, a swimming pool, village greens and a charming museum, all beautifully integrated into the site. It is an absolute 'must visit' place, especially in the summer.

Derek and I had performed at the theatre previously, but on this occasion, one particular regression case stood out from the rest and is worthy of inclusion in this chapter. This regression was so filled with emotion and such a great amount of clear detail that, after the demonstration, Derek and I decided to research and film the results.

It was here that I met Mr Mike Boyd, a care worker from Wallasey. I regressed him back through the passage of time to 11 November 1735, in the city of Gloucester, England, UK. His name in this past life was Jack Mahon. Jack was 18 years of age, and from first contact, he spoke with a completely different dialect, in keeping with folk from that part of England, yet very different from his usual voice. Jack worked for a company named H. & Sons and lived in a house on Skinner Street in the city. There were no numbers on the houses there and his house was described only by the colour of its door. Derek interacted well with Jack throughout the regression and the following further information was received.

Jack had taken a fancy to a young lady named Mary Jane Smith and, at the age of twenty, they married and had one son, John, named after his grandfather. At the age of four, John had developed a walking difficulty which was never rectified. They were a religious family and attended the local Church of England church. Jack had no official schooling but received some education as a child at the church and from two people he called Father James and Sister Anne. Throughout the regression, Jack's playful character became very obvious. Sister Anne did not like frogs and during one Sunday service he placed a frog on the pew next to her. The result was exactly what Jack had anticipated – screams and uproar. At certain times, for reasons we didn't discover in the dialogue, Jack was punished by *birching* – sometimes known as whipping or flogging. This punishment was widely used at that period in history, and it was still being used in the Isle of Man up until January 1976, when I was a child. People on the mainland kept writing to the papers about how effective it was to thrash kids with 'the birch' and asking for it to be brought back!

Information regarding his work at H. & Sons revealed discrepancies with their accounts, and Jack's position within the company was what would be described today as a stocktaker. Jack had discovered that commodities on the docks were not tallying with inventories and this led, as it usually does, to conflict with the workers he was associated with. Overall, I believe that Jack lived a happy life. Towards the end of the regression, I instructed him to travel within the timeline of this incarnation to his eventual passing. In his last few moments, his breathing slowed and his body calmed dramatically. During the whole regression, his hands had been shaking, but now, in these final moments, his body began to settle, and he became very peaceful. Jack died at home while his wife Mary tended to him. Derek, who was very intensely focussed on the situation, picked up a strange fragrance – possibly of an old form of disinfectant that may have been used – and then, just at the moment of passing, he also picked up the presence of an old lady, possibly his mother in spirit form.

Mike's body was buried in his local churchyard.

Postscript

We were in possession of so much material that a decision was made to investigate further, and so arrangements were made with Square One Pictures, under the guidance of producer Roger DaSilva and the watchful eyes of New York film director, Chase Johnston Lynch, to travel to the city of Gloucester with the subject, Mike Boyd. Some research was conducted before our travel and we discovered that the church, Skinner Street and H. & Sons had existed in the year 1735, and the business continued to trade.

It was all getting very interesting. As we entered Skinner Street on foot, Mike became rather emotional. Our research concluded that Mike's home had been demolished, but he did not know this at the time and had a déjà vu feeling when he stood in Skinner Street, pointing out where his house once stood. This proved correct, too, according to the plans at the local archives.

Mike experienced a sensation of being drawn to the old abbey. Here, he pointed out that all the graves had been removed in 1800. This gave him feelings of a past soul progression to the present day, linking his past life to the present one.

This raises the question: 'Do those souls from our past lives also link in with our present soul?' Efforts to find the grave were dashed when we discovered a lot of the graves were lost and buildings had been developed on the former burial grounds.

This was really satisfying to me. In my view, this is what past life regression is all about, not just a grunt and groan, the name of a country, and the name of a husband or wife. This is the meat on the bones, verifying against all odds the proof of the spirit or soul progressing from generation to generation.

Regression Four

This is my final story of regression, so join me as we visit Liverpool, a world famous city, and rightly so, with its diverse cultures, its friendly inhabitants, great history, and, of course, The Beatles.

The date is 18 April 2012, and I was invited by my friend, Anna Harrison, to give a private regression to one of her friends, who I will name Edward. Edward is a serving police officer in North Wales but he resides on the Wirral, just a few miles west of Liverpool, and commutes across the English - Welsh border, to and from his work. I had not met Edward before but he struck me as a nice gentleman, well mannered, of sound mind, and very professional.

Edward entered into a trance state very quickly and his communication was very clear and audible. He rapidly regressed back to a lifetime that was lived near the dockland in Liverpool, in the year 1902. His incarnate name here was John Pritchard. He gave his address as 5 Cuthbert Street, Liverpool, and he was aged twenty-seven at the point of contact. John was married to Brenda, two years his junior, and he described himself as an abusive and violent alcoholic. His local pub was The Cross Foxes.

During his early childhood, he attended the school of St. Mary's, and although a Catholic, did not go to church or follow his religion. Money was very scarce and, looking back, the working classes had it so very much harder in those days, in comparison to what we have experienced in current times. His parents were John and Margaret. Even as a young child, he was very unhappy. There were no children born from this marriage to Brenda and, as time progressed, he became more violent and abusive to his wife. It was not a happy existence; from childhood to old age, the poverty was crippling.

John was a docker, or *stevedore*, and his job was to unload wool from the ships into boxes. Now, during the regression, I had noticed he was continually rubbing and scratching his arms. He explained that the wool constantly itched his arms and that his arms and hands were always red raw.

Then, towards the end of the regression, I guided him to the last hour of this existence. He described the scene up to his last breath, aged 68, a doctor and his wife present to hear his last words as he lay in bed at his home. His liver was shot with the ravages of alcoholism, and he felt that Brenda would surely be relieved that he had gone.

I had one more final question: 'Where is your body buried?' He replied, 'In a churchyard in South Allerton, Liverpool, and the headstone is near to a tree.'

Postscript

I left Edward after the session, but not before we chatted briefly on what I had experienced during the regression. He remembered nothing at all and was a little taken aback when I recapped on his past life.

I recorded the whole regression for Edward to take home with him. Since then, he has conducted his own research into the life of 'John Pritchard' and has confirmed that virtually the whole regression was verifiable. However, the one thing that he cannot find is the final resting place – his grave.

Edward is a very proud Welshman, but he told me something very interesting. 'Every time I travel into the city of Liverpool, I have a strange feeling of coming home.'

Note: After touring for several years and regressing thousands of people, I have collected many audio recordings, and a small edited sample of them are available to listen to live on my regression website – www.pastlives.tv. I do hope you enjoy them.

10. Real People – Real Lives

Looking back at my life in general and my professional career has really led me to believe that there are some very strange people living amongst us. Apart from the statistical fact, according to the media, that one in every hundred people living in the UK has the potential to develop psychopathic tendencies, I have certainly met far more of my share of weird and wonderful folk, and the true tales I tell may be hard to swallow but one thing that I have learned in life is 'always expect the unexpected'. In other words, what you think can never ever happen, probably will!

In the nineties, my hypnotic cabaret show was keeping me very busy and I was driving the length and breadth of the UK several times each week. On several occasions, I returned by popular request to certain theatres and clubs and my popularity, partly due to guest spots on national television shows, gave me the opportunity to build up a fan club. On one particular occasion, I was to return to a cabaret club in Shropshire, England.

At the end of the performance, and after a nice cup of tea, I was dismantling my PA sound system and carrying it out to my car when I noticed a young, female police officer observing me.

There was nobody else around as the audience had now dispersed and gone home. She walked over, smiled and introduced herself. I will name her Susan. Susan had attended one of my *comedy* shows on a previous visit to the locality and admitted that she loved, and was intrigued by, my work, and she asked me for an autograph. After chatting with her for about ten minutes I said I needed to leave, due to the staff wanting to close up and go home, and I needed to finish packing away my equipment.

Susan again asked for an autograph. I said sure, but I didn't have a pen and my picture cards for signing were packed away. Susan said it was no problem, she would like me to sign her breasts instead. I nearly fell over with shock and told her she must be joking. Susan was looking all around and over her shoulder as she undid her police uniform tunic. She passed me a black pen and said, 'Quickly, just put 'To Susan, love Alan.' And a kiss.'!

The author with Graham Norton

I have to admit it was the best autograph I have ever given, and she did possess a perfectly formed pair of beautiful breasts.

Target

In 2012, I had the privilege to perform at the Fringe Comedy Festival in Jakarta, Indonesia, which gave me the opportunity to work alongside some of the very best and most famous comedians in the world. The headline act was Bill Bailey, a guy I have admired for many years. A lot of people know his work from the TV but I can assure you that his live shows are even more amazing.

During our stage and sound check rehearsals, I was sharing the stage with Indonesia's famous magician and crazy illusionist, Deddy Corbuzier. Deddy had set up a large backdrop and when I asked him what he was using it for he replied, 'It's for my knife throwing routine.' He then asked if he could practise on me. And here I have to say that he must have hypnotised me – the hypnotist! – because, immediately, without any hesitation at all I replied, 'Yes, sure.'

The author with Deddy Corbuzier (top) and at press event with Bill Bailey (above), Jakarta Fringe Comedy Festival, 2012

The next moment I found myself stood against the board and within seconds – bang, bang, bang, bang – four very sharp knives were embedded in the solid backdrop. Of these trembling blades, two of them were a centimetre away from each of my temples. The other two were equally as near to my 'privates'.

I don't ever want to see a knife that close down there ever again. I came out of my 'trance' state very quickly thinking, 'What on earth did I say "yes" for?' And as I walked away from the board it was rapidly and graphically dawning on me that if I had moved just a fraction, it would have been fatal.

The knives in the picture were positioned later for the camera pose. I later sold the rights of my show to Indonesian television and consequently my show was edited, subtitled and broadcast nationally, I believe, throughout Indonesia.

The Skill of the Hypnotist

Similar to lots of professions, there is an incredible amount to learn before presenting comedy hypnosis on stage. Nothing in the theatre is ever as easy as it seems. I practised for many years to make it look relaxed and simple, but I assure you it isn't.

Firstly, there is the element of putting volunteers into a trance state, and never mind how talented you are as an entertainer, this involves a great deal of skill just to 'see' how each individual is responding to the suggestions the hypnotist makes. The hypnotist must also notice the levels that they are capable of being taken to, and of course where they are at, at any given moment. This is very important in that there are several people 'in trance' at any time. Some are impossible to even help to relax whereas others drop into very deep states as I walk towards them. I sometimes think that, in the right situation, if I coughed they would go under.

Secondly, it is just as important to understand how to end a show and remove all traces of hypnosis carefully, and again with plenty of attention to the participants as they come out of trance and back to the 'real' world, before you can allow them to leave the stage.

Everybody can make mistakes. However, if you learn from your mistakes you are becoming better for it, and this is the way we humans have progressed for millions of years. I'm sure the discovery of fire and the first ape that came down from the trees was making a 'mistake' – while also taking a great step forward.

The next tale had slipped from my memory until a friend reminded me. In 2004, I was booked to perform at a holiday camp in North Wales, UK. The show was a thank-you party arranged by the owners for all the staff at the end of a busy season, and they had provided a sit-down hot dinner, band, comedy hypnotist show and a disco. I was introduced on stage by the camp's compere and all of the staff were in very 'high spirits' and, shall we say, slightly inebriated due to the free drinks that were on offer. I managed to amass my usual twelve willing stars on stage and, after a quick psychological induction, reduced the number to about five deeply hypnotised subjects. I performed well for about an hour and everything felt as if it was going well.

One of my popular routines at the time involved men's dress ties. I suggested under hypnosis to one middle-aged guy that the event he was attending was a formal occasion and that he was not wearing a tie. I then suggested he should come to me and I would give him a tie, and then he would go and sit back down in the audience. Of course, as soon as he sat down with his tie on, the suggestion would immediately take effect and he would jump up and believe he was improperly dressed, dashing back again to the stage, apologising profusely to everyone for his incorrect dress, asking if there was by any chance a spare tie available? And 'what a surprise', I just happened to have one ...

As you can imagine, this was a very funny sketch, the audience witnessing a gentleman who genuinely believed he was underdressed yet had ten kipper ties from the 1960s fashion era around his neck. To finish the sketch, I cancelled the suggestion for more ties but left the hideous coloured ties on him until the very end of the show, though of course he was left totally unaware of their presence, and what a snappy dresser he looked until then. At the very end of the show, I removed the suggestions from the minds of the other stars on stage but forgot to do so with 'kipper tie man'.

Then, two days later, I received a call from the club's general manager requesting that I speak to the kipper tie man, as his wife had made contact due to him having an embarrassing problem. Before going to bed, he was going backwards and forwards into his wardrobe and putting on his dress ties! I agreed on a time to visit and the next day I travelled back to North Wales and visited him at his home. He was very susceptible to hypnosis and I was able to put him into a deep trance easily within five minutes. I then cleared all the suggestions from the comedy show and, I am glad to report, his wife contacted me a week later to inform me all was going well. So, another lesson was learned: always be thorough when closing down a session of comedy hypnosis.

Which brings me to an important question that I have been asked many times and which I always take very seriously.

Question: Alan, have you ever misused the power of hypnosis?

Answer: You decide.

I personally would say no, I have never misused hypnosis. But, in my early days, I did do some silly things that, looking back now, could be considered humiliating by some.

The Guy that Called Shark

In the late nineties, I went on a lads' holiday to Tenerife in the beautiful Spanish Canary Islands. Altogether, there were twelve of us, all eager to party and have lots of fun.

One of our party members had a gay friend who lived in London who worked as cabin crew and flew with British airways. I will name him Troy, for privacy's sake. Troy joined the rest of us a couple of days later due to his shift pattern and was made very welcome by our band of heterosexual males. Troy was very effeminate in his mannerisms but had an amazing sense of humour which brightened up our days no end.

One afternoon we were all sunbathing around the hotel's swimming pool. The sun was cracking the flags and as it was so incredibly hot it was a natural response to dip into the pool to cool down every fifteen minutes or so. Troy was sunbathing next to me and was very inquisitive regarding my work as a hypnotist. After chatting for over an hour, he asked me if I would mind hypnotising him as he wanted to experience this altered state of awareness. I agreed, on condition that we may have a bit of fun at his expense.

So, within minutes, Troy was in a deep trance state, helped by the natural idyllic setting and, of course, the beautiful climate. By now the rest of the guys, like vultures, had gathered around Troy's sun lounger, and it was becoming time to decide upon what fate Troy would endure for the afternoon's poolside entertainment.

It was decided, as a group choice, that the next time Troy was to take a dip in the pool to cool down, a suggestion was to be placed into his subconscious that a very hungry great white shark was waiting in the swimming pool for some poor soul and his duty would be to scream and shout at all the other swimmers to vacate the pool immediately, if not sooner, or face the consequences and probably be eaten alive. As the pool was shared by lots of other holidaymakers, we were fairly sure this would liven up our afternoon.

The guys were now all back on their sunbeds, apparently all relaxing and enjoying the peace and tranquillity, and Troy was none the wiser about what had been 'planted' into his subconscious. And, obviously to all, he had really enjoyed the soothing sleepy state that I had induced in him. He was completely unaware that I had given him a trigger word which was quite simply **'SHARK'**. Upon this activating trigger word, Troy was instructed to literally freak out in the pool and scream 'Shark attack!' as loud as possible at all the swimmers, breaking the peace and tranquillity of their restful afternoon.

Shortly after, Troy sat up, stretched his muscles and said he was off to cool down in the pool. The guys all sat bolt upright on their loungers and awaited his fate. Troy, still completely oblivious of the rising charge of expectancy in the air, entered the pool gently and quietly. I let the tension mount for as long as I felt I could, milking the situation and the 'audience' shamelessly. After a couple of minutes, I discreetly whispered 'SHARK'. None of us could have expected the reaction which Troy gave to this trigger word.

You have to remember, dear reader, that his subconscious could now see this very large 'great white' lurking in the pool, licking his lips and grinning from gill to gill, all in very real and very intense detail. Some folk have very powerful imaginations, and I think Troy did – in fact, I'm sure he did because he proved it that very afternoon.

The air was suddenly ripped apart by a highly charged, highly pitched sound, a piping wail rising as I don't think I have ever heard before. He flung his head back and let rip at the top of his reedy warbling voice. People were paralysed by it. Mothers covered their ears. Diving kids stopped in mid-air. Some of the lads even stopped drinking.

Then there was silence for about four seconds, which really felt to me like an hour. And then that voice came again. Just as loud, and just as certain – though also terrified for everybody's safety. I had to admire him. 'Everybody out the pool! OUT! NOW! Shark attack! SHARK! Quickly, you are all going to be eaten alive, get out. Get out, now,' he screamed, 'or you will all die!'

Well, the look on the faces of the twenty or so swimmers was a picture. They were totally unaware of what Troy was enduring. Several of them rushed to get out of the water, while others stood rigid while trying to process what was happening. Troy was so adamant that a shark was going to eat the swimmers that I dived into the pool and commanded him to sleep. It was the only thing I could have done. He had reacted, from his point of view, so well. And I knew that upon waking all would be well and he would have no recollection of the event.

Hula-Hula Dancer from Manchester

My next tale takes us to Manchester, England. Manchester is a great city and, not unlike Liverpool, its inhabitants are friendly, welcoming and possess a good sense of humour. I spent quite a lot of time performing shows in Manchester and made several friends, of both the male and female varieties. So, whenever I was in town, arrangements were made for after-show parties, and a restaurant that we often frequented was the well-known Shere Khan on the 'Curry Mile', in a part of the city named Rushholme.

One of our group was a pretty girl that I will name Jaz. Now, Jaz was a nightclub dancer and always attended my shows and after-show parties whenever possible. She was also, as it turns out, extremely susceptible to hypnosis. I found this out one evening during a show at a university, during the famous 'freshers' week' tour.

Another of those 'questions' that I often get asked is, 'Is it possible to tell if a person is susceptible to hypnosis upon meeting them, before an attempt is made?'

Now, my answer for many years was no, not until you try an induction first. However, I have now changed my view, as very often upon meeting a stranger I have developed an ability to determine if they can be hypnotised. It is a feeling that I get when I am talking with them about the subject of hypnosis, though I have to say that it doesn't always work 100 per cent.

It was during the university show that I noticed Jaz falling asleep every time I said the word 'sleep', and she was not even participating in the show. As weeks passed, I noticed that sometimes, if I looked at her a certain way, she would faint. I had to be very careful with her as she was very sensitive, but I always had her best interests at heart, honestly. Well, apart from one evening at the Shere Khan.

One Saturday evening after a show, about fifteen of us had a late supper and everybody was in very jovial spirits. I was in a mischievous mood so I made a discrete suggestion to Jaz that she was a Hawaiian hula dancer and that the next time the waiter attended our table she would stand on her chair and dance. When the waiter arrived with more poppadoms, this professional dancer, with curves in all the right places, went up on to the chair and entertained the whole restaurant. Afterwards, to the delight of our party, I suggested to her she would remember nothing at all of the dance.

Susceptibility

As I was just writing about the ability to sense a person's susceptibility to hypnosis, another memory popped into my head. In 2013, I was engaged to perform at a restaurant in Leicestershire, England. It was very badly organised, which happens sometimes, no matter how hard one tries to get everything set like clockwork. There was absolutely no promotion, nor any opening nor commencement times given, which is essential for all events to be anything like successful. I mean, people didn't even know when to turn up for the show.

So I went through the motions and managed to make the best out of a poor night. Now, before I started work, we were given a meal and the waitress that served us displayed traits that felt to me indicated she would make a good star for the show. Unfortunately, this never materialised as she was on duty and that was the end of that thought process. However, just before I left the venue, I had an invoice that needed to be paid, so I joined a small group of staff that were also waiting to receive their wages. This waitress was now standing just in front of me. She then turned and asked, 'Can you hypnotise me here, and now?'

I would normally have made an excuse as I had a long drive home, but on this occasion I instantly grabbed her hand, turned her around in a fast spinning motion and slapped her hand onto a solid wall. I then suggested to her that her hand was glued to the wall and that she would not be able to move it in any way, shape or form. The small group around us in the queue were now mesmerised at what I had just done and the sheer speed of it. Even though she was in front of me in the queue, I left her stuck to the wall until I had received my fee.

On walking out, she was desperately struggling to take her hand off the wall. I simply walked up, in view of all her friends, and ever so gently lifted her hand off the wall, kissed it, and bid her goodnight.

Cyril Sausage

Accrington Stanley is a small village in Lancashire, England, thirty-two miles north of Manchester. I was booked to entertain at a Christmas office party for a local building supplies company, and leading by example for volunteers was the owner of the company who, for confidential reasons, I will name John. John was a lively, enthusiastic middle-aged man, and he was eager to be hypnotised. As it transpired, he was the star of the performance that night – to the delight of his staff and the rest of the audience.

Workers love to see the boss getting some stick and during the show I told him his name was now Cyril – Cyril Sausage, to be precise. I told him that he would bet any amount of money that his name was not John but Cyril and the only name he would respond to for the duration of the sketch was Cyril. I snapped my fingers and Cyril's eyes opened. You now have to visualise the scenario here. I was chatting to him and opened naturally enough with, 'Hello, John, it's nice to meet you.'

He looked at me very confused and replied, 'I am sorry but my name is not John, it's Cyril. Cyril Sausage.'

You could not script or act the look on his face. Meanwhile, his employees were doubled up with laughter. So I then put on a mutual bet with him for £20 that his name was John. As fast as lightening, out came his wallet and a crisp £20 note. 'I will certainly bet on my name being Cyril,' he responded without a second's hesitation.

I took his money but put him instantly back to sleep and told him he had completely forgotten about the twenty pounds and his name was now back to John – the £20 now very safely tucked away in my pocket. Upon waking him again, I referred to him as Cyril Sausage and he said, 'I think you are talking about another person. My name is John.'

So this was the end of the sketch and I continued with the show, though I still had his £20 note, tucked away and safe. Now, usually at the end of the show, most of the audience, and especially the star of the show, have forgotten about the money, so I take this opportunity and present him with the £20 and say, 'It's been great to meet you tonight, and I would like to buy you and your friends a drink.'

And then I give him back his own money. The look of glee on their face is one of gratitude and happiness in believing they had just been given money for nothing.

Sadly, for some unknown reason, in this show, I completely forgot to give him back his money and it wasn't until my agent rang me the next day and enquired if I had the twenty that belonged to the show's organiser? I was mortified. I posted a cheque off that very same day to reimburse him, with a letter of apology and a big thank you for the show booking.

Many times I have performed when the show booker, manager or owner of the venue has been the star of the show – some unwittingly, and some very consciously and sportingly. And, afterwards, when I have asked for my fee, I have been told, 'Yes, sure, Alan. After you have been on stage.' Likewise, it has been known for me to suggest to the bar manager to buy all the regular customers a free drink after I have left the venue.

Every entertainer is always hungry for publicity, and I am, I suppose, no different. As Oscar Wilde stated, 'There is only one thing worse than being talked about, and that is **NOT** being talked about.' And in my case it is certainly completely true. As a young developing comedy stage hypnotist, I was asked by my bank manager to try and help him give up smoking. So here I am sitting in the bank manager's office, the manager is in a deep trance, the bank staff have all left for home, and a thought has popped into my mind ... in fact, several, and all of them involving me struggling from the premises with either one, two or perhaps three great big bags.

Of course, when I weighed up publicity versus time in jail, it didn't stack up. And as I am a truly honest man, anyway, I chose freedom. (It was only a thought, by the way.)

Hypnotising My Own Stage Manager

The saying is very true: *you learn as you go along.* I learned at an early stage of my development never to employ a stage manager/technician who is susceptible to hypnosis. My dear friend DJ Trix accompanied me to Great Yarmouth in Norfolk, England, to assist as my stage manager and sound operator at a once famous club named The Garibaldi.

DJ Trix is a very talented man, world famous in his own right, and was once crowned European mixing champion. He promoted Vestax audio products worldwide and was flown into gigs in Japan by helicopter – in other words, someone who has really enjoyed the high-life. I was stuck once for a technician as my regular guy, Andy, was not available, so Trix offered to travel with me and assist. I will explain, before I go any further, that Trix was on the same deeply susceptible level as Jaz, the dancer from Manchester, mentioned earlier, and I had failed to think this all through properly beforehand.

Once we reached The Garibaldi club we sound checked and waited for our call time to start the show, all of which went well. In fact it wasn't until I had my volunteers from the audience up on the stage and hypnotised that I realised that I had a problem. I had already suggested that on the count of three they would be wide awake and play an invisible piano, when it came home to me. It was at this point that Trix would have started the sketch music, which was Nina Simone's 'My Baby Just Cares for Me', but there was no music. Just silence. Though I was preoccupied with all the other elements of the show, I knew that something was not happening and not right. I turned to look back at the sound control mixer and poor Trix was slumped over it – fast asleep! And this continued through each routine. But, fortunately, the audience were kind to me and saw the funny side of it when I explained the situation. I adapted the show by improvising the routines and the end result was good, and certainly spontaneous – but very different.

Do I Ever Get an Audience Where Nobody Was Hypnotised?

Not every show goes to plan and a question I get asked on occasion is, 'Do I ever get a show audience when nobody is hypnotised?' The answer to that is of course, but thankfully it is very, very few and far between. The times this has happened – and I don't think I'm passing the buck here – has been when things have been out of my control, such as bad venue promotion, when only ten people have turned up for the show because, as I mentioned earlier, no one informed them that I was even there. That is very disheartening. But then there are audiences that just do not respond; I can't be everyone's cup of tea, after all. And then there are some times that you get an uninterested audience or an audience that has the concentration span of a fruit fly.

I can remember returning from a tour with the famous thalidomide comedian Gary Skyner. We had completed a red-carpet tour of the Gulf States and very successfully launched The Laughter Factory agency in Dubai. The night I landed back in the UK, I was to perform at a club in darkest Liverpool. I arrived at the venue, which was the dirtiest, scruffiest place I have ever set foot in, a place where you needed to wipe your feet on the way out. It was full of undesirables, skinheads openly smoking dope at the tables, and when I started the show nobody even looked at the stage. It was as if I wasn't even there. Thank goodness it doesn't happen at all frequently because when it does your heart just drops. Such is the life of an entertainer, going from one extreme to another.

Bang!

Saturday, 7 December 2002 was an interesting show. I had been booked to perform at the Tower Arts Centre, Winchester, England. I duly arrived to find to my disappointment that they had only sold thirty tickets. To make things worse for me, though without wishing to sound disrespectful, the audience that arrived were all elderly with grey hair and hearing aids. If you know that the audience is going to be like that, and of that age range or disabled, you can prepare for it and make it work. This night, it was a complete surprise.

As a professional entertainer, the show must go on, so at my appointed time of 8.00 pm, I made my musical stage entrance and, just as I stepped onto the stage wondering how I could slant the show to appeal to this audience, and in this venue – and also thinking that it just could not get any worse –BANG! The venue's sound system blew up. I'm usually a lucky person, but this night I began to think that this show was just not meant to be. But I persevered and took the show more to them, making it more direct and straightforward. Within a fairly short time, I had the audience 100 per cent on my side. They did as I asked them and, lo and behold, I managed to hypnotise four terrific subjects. When I explained to them that at certain stages of the show different pieces of music would play, the audience took it on themselves to improvise and *sing* the routines. I ended up giving a wonderful show that evening and the memory is still with me.

Gary Skyner

I have just mentioned my dear friend Gary Skyner, the comedian. I think the next story deserves to be featured here, reprinted from my autobiography, Wide Awake. In August 2009, Gary and I travelled to the Middle East to tour the Arabian Gulf states, including Dubai, Al Ain, Sharjah, Doha, Abu Dhabi and Bahrain. I returned to tour Dubai every year afterwards for the following ten years.

Gary was born disabled with very short arms and missing fingers due to the disastrous effects of the drug thalidomide, which was prescribed in the 1950s to expectant mothers for morning sickness.

Gary's opening line on stage at our very first show was, 'Good evening, ladies and gentlemen, and welcome to the Hyatt Hotel. It's nice to be here in Dubai, but it's the last time I go f*****g shoplifting!' *(Insinuating the authorities had cut his arms off for stealing).* Gary lifted the roof off the ballroom with the applause he received, he was such a joy to be around; he exuded happiness and laughter everywhere he went, on and off the stage.

While we were shopping at a mall, Gary directed my attention to a particular store, The Body Shop, looking through the window and beckoning me in. As soon as I entered, I instantly knew he was up to no good. There were two pretty young Asian girls serving behind the counter and when they saw Gary their jaws dropped. Thalidomide was covered up in the Middle East and it would have been their first experience of seeing a victim. When Gary broke the silence and asked them for 'two elbows and three fingers please,' the poor girls were totally speechless.

Gary said to them with a straight face, 'What's wrong, ladies? This is the Body Shop, isn't it?'

11. The Rendlesham Forest UFO

I have already published this amazing story in my last book, Wide Awake. It is that incredible and so very different to all the other examples of my work that I believe it also belongs in this book, too. So, whatever your belief system, please keep an open mind here because something very strange did happen on that cold winter's night a long time ago.

The incident occurred in 1980, in late December, and the location was Rendlesham Forest, in Suffolk, England. Nearby RAF Woodbridge was a base utilised by the American Air Force, and it was here that what many people consider to be the UK's most fascinating UFO incident took place. Events that happened here were on the scale of America's famous 'Roswell' which, even today, after 69 years, still draws plenty of attention.

I do not endeavour to cover this story in complete detail but rather only the salient points relevant to my experience. For the interested reader, it's worth spending time researching this incident as it is a fascinating story in itself, and thirty-six years later, not unlike Roswell, it is still a magnet for those with a passion for this particular kind of unexplained phenomena.

At 3 a.m. on 26 December 1980, strange lights were reported by a security patrol near the East Gate of RAF Woodbridge, apparently descending into nearby Rendlesham Forest. Servicemen initially thought it was a downed aircraft, but upon entering the forest to investigate they saw – according to the Deputy Base Lt. Col. Charles Halt's memo: a strange glowing object, metallic in appearance, with coloured lights. As they approached, it moved through the trees, and 'the animals on a nearby farm went into a frenzy'. The craft left three impressions, or depressions, in the ground, which were visible the next day. One of the servicemen, Sergeant Jim Penniston, allegedly claimed to have encountered a 'craft of unknown origin' and to have made detailed notes of its features, touched its 'warm' surface, and copied the numerous symbols on its body. The object reportedly flew away after their brief encounter. Shortly after 4 a.m., local British police were called to the scene but reported that the only lights they could see were those from the lighthouse some miles away on the coast.

Sometime after daybreak on the morning of 26 December, servicemen returned to a small clearing near the eastern edge of the forest and found three small impressions in a triangular pattern, as well as burn marks and broken branches on nearby trees. At 10.30 a.m., the local police were called out again, this time to see the impressions on the ground. Several servicemen and Lt. Col. Charles Halt returned to the site again in the early hours of 28th December with radiation detectors. Halt investigated this sighting personally and recorded the events on a micro-cassette recorder. It was during this investigation that a flashing light was seen across the field to the east, almost in line with a farmhouse. The Orford Ness lighthouse is visible further to the east in the same line of sight. Later, star-like lights were seen in the sky to the north and south, the brightest of which seemed to beam down a stream of light from time to time. There are claims that the incident was videoed by the U.S. Air Force; but, if so, the resulting tape has not yet been made public.

Thirty years later I was approached by Paul Wookey, a TV presenter and film-maker with a keen interest in the paranormal. Paul had gathered a team that included Lt. Col. Charles Halt (USAF, retired deputy base commander), Nick Pope[1], formerly the UK Ministry of Defence's own UFO 'X-files' style investigator (1985 to 2006), TV presenter Emily Booth, the psychic medium, Christine Hamlett Walsh, and myself. The objective was to produce a TV documentary and to try and uncover what really happened on those dark nights in December 1980. By utilising all of our talents we hoped to probe deeper and, once and for all, resolve the file on Rendlesham on its 30th anniversary.

Apart from the United States military witnesses, there are other local English witnesses who claim not only to have seen what is already out in the public domain, but also to have actually been abducted and still to be in contact with their abductors. My input in this exciting documentary was to hypnotise and regress a local lady named Brenda.

Brenda seriously believes that aliens regularly make contact with her. She was willing for me to hypnotise her and regress her to this time period, and also – if permission was granted under hypnosis – to communicate with her alien associates. This was the first time I was to do something like this. I was very excited with the prospect of involving hypnosis in the investigation, and also of speaking with an 'alien' by using a human as a host. To me, something had happened that night that must have been extraordinary – beyond the ordinary – and I was very interested in finding out what it could be.

---

1   Nick Pope, Encounter in Rendlesham Forest

We conducted the session at Brenda's home. Once the production team and cameramen were set to go, I successfully hypnotised the subject and guided her into a very deep trance state. Brenda relived her first close encounter and abduction in the forest and this was really fascinating to listen to. This was similar in many ways to past life regression – notes were being taken, and video and audio records were being made to catch any verifiable evidence that the witness can relate to be collaborated later. But what happened next gave me a jolt. Under deep hypnosis I asked if it were possible for me to communicate with her alien associate. Brenda's voice paused for a minute and then she spoke. Permission was granted and, from that point, I was 'allegedly' communicating with an entity from another world. Just as when I had hypnotised medium Gary Dakin during the trance séance, the synchronising of the actual voice box with the muscles in the mouth and throat where not in tune or alignment. It is possible for humans to do this voluntarily but very difficult; you would really have to practice. To give you an example of what I witnessed, it was like watching a good ventriloquist doing very unnatural things yet producing a natural though disassociated flow of words, if you can understand. Here, the voice was completely different to Brenda's and had a character and an atmosphere all its own.

The dialogue itself was interesting too. The alien informed us that they had been on Earth for centuries and that there were two types of species, which were basically at war with each other. The entity assured me that they were the peaceful ones and that the host, Brenda, was safe to be used in such a manner, though for a limited time only. My final question to the alien was, 'Were you responsible for the activity in Rendlesham Forest, in December 1980?' The reply was distinctly affirmative! The several other elements of the programme contained fascinating first-hand accounts with Lt. Col. Charles Halt. This man held the highest security clearance at the time with the United States Air Force, and Nick Pope likewise held UK security MOD clearance.

At exactly the same time and date thirty years later, our team gathered in Rendlesham Forest at the same location to recall step by step from Lt. Col. Halt what really happened. There are several conspiracy theories, including the accusation of a cover-up by the US and UK military. And then here we have Lt. Col. Halt, in my opinion a man of very sound mind, intelligent and articulate, recounting exactly what happened thirty years ago on this very night.

Nick Pope, Brenda, the author and Lt. Col. Charles Holt

One of the theories put forward is that the USAF were using the airbase as a storage facility for nuclear weapons, contrary to a clear denial from both the UK and US governments. I put this question to Lt. Col. Halt off camera but he refused to answer. My personal feelings are that, yes, this was a storage base for WMD, or 'Weapons of Mass Destruction', which, at the time of the intense confrontations at Greenham Common, would have certainly, explained the secrecy. The nuclear weapons scenario has also been suggested as the reason for possible alien interest in the area.

Another theory is that the light they saw was the light emanating from the Orford Ness lighthouse. During our filming, the cloud visibility and weather was fair and we could clearly see the beam of light from the lighthouse. I can categorically state that in those conditions, they were nothing like the lights witnessed in 1980. The Orford light was a tiny blip in the distance and, to me, it is complete nonsense to put this theory forward.

The Rendlesham Forest incident sadly still remains a mystery and may never be solved. But, for me, I greatly enjoyed meeting and working with Lt. Col. Halt, Nick Pope and my other colleagues, and spending time on the film shoot, including my experiences with the alleged abductee, Brenda. These incidents and experiences themselves 'open' our minds to new viewpoints and to question the nature of what we accept as 'normal'. It is my personal view that a cover-up had taken place at Rendlesham Forest and that we, mere mortals, are being shielded. But, if so, why, and for what purpose? The following information made news headlines in 2015.

US airman John Burroughs secured the settlement after years of trying to prove his ill-health was caused by the encounter in Rendlesham Forest.

A former Ministry of Defence (MoD) official said the pay-out confirms that what he saw was real and had caused him physical harm.

Mr Burroughs put forward a declassified report as evidence he had been injured during the event on Boxing Day 1980.

He said disability coverage from the US Veteran's Association offered 'some closure', but that he now wanted unrestricted access to his full medical records.

'Every step along the way people have said it's not true. Some people will always say that.

'I don't know if I have the full answer, but no one thought I'd get this far,' said the ex-servicemen. Along with Jim Penniston, he was the first to investigate mysterious lights near the East Gate of RAF Woodbridge.

Theories included the glow of Orfordness Lighthouse, an elaborate hoax and a secret classified aircraft.

Lawyer Pat Frascogna, who represented the retired technical sergeant, said: 'This excludes the bogus explanations put out there over the years. I cannot underscore what a major development this is. We're more curious now than ever.

'We were denied access to records, mainly dating back to 1979, which we believe would have shown John had no health problems when he entered the air force, but that he developed heart problems and other ailments that arose from the incident.'

In fighting his case, Mr Burroughs used a declassified study code-named Project Condign, in which Rendlesham is described as an event where it 'might be postulated that several observers were probably exposed to Unidentified Aerial Phenomena (UAP) radiation.'

Mr Frascogna said: 'Condign specifically mentions the incident and how radiation from unidentified aerial phenomena could cause injury.

'John was able to furnish that document, and another dating back to the incident, when a radiation reading found levels to be significantly higher than normal.'

Mr Burroughs, who suffers heart problems and has a pacemaker, said: 'I'm very happy we finally have some closure.

'Condign explained that there is a phenomenon that governments of this world are well aware of. The question is where it comes from.'

Four years ago, the MoD released 35 archives of UFO-

related documents but then revealed that papers on Rendlesham had gone missing. Mr Burroughs believes the missing files may reveal further clues.

Nick Pope, author of Encounter in Rendlesham Forest: The Inside Story of the World's Best-Documented UFO Incident, worked on the government's UFO desk in the early 1990s.

He said: 'After years of denial this is official confirmation that what they encountered was real, and caused them physical harm.

'This welcome development doesn't give us a definitive explanation of the Rendlesham Forest incident, but it takes us ever closer to the truth.'

12. Bizarre Therapy

This part of the book is dedicated to some of my additional notable successes in bizarre therapy cases. Rest assured, reader, confidentiality is, as ever, of paramount importance at all times, and no client here will be compromised.

Merry Christmas

Christmas for most Christians is a time for celebration, Baby Jesus, the nativity, Santa Claus, gifts and, of course, great parties all round. In my next story, though, Christmas is a complete disaster and a psychologically damaging time of the year for my young client, whom I shall name Samantha.

Samantha is a typical sixteen-year-old teenager; that is, she is normal and everyday up to and until the Christmas period – and then things go seriously wrong. Samantha was brought to see me by her parents several years ago, as this strange behaviour was not only ruining the family Christmas but was extremely upsetting for Samantha herself.

Once we were seated in my office I slowly started to gather all the pieces I needed to put the mental jigsaw together in my mind. With simple questions and gentle probing, and a great deal of careful listening, piece by piece the picture of the problem can then become fleshed out and apparent. Often what I see is not the same as how the client first describes it or thinks of it, and the real cause emerges slowly, as in this case.

My early observations led me to believe that the parents were partly to blame for Sam's psychological problems. They reminded me of Gomez and Morticia from the TV series *The Addams Family*. I needed to get to the root of the problem and, if you can visualise the following dialogue, it will better put you in a position to follow my reasoning, bearing in mind that I was like you at this point, still with no idea as to why they had come seeking help. There is a wonderful openness and mystery about the opening of a case like this, or any such therapy case, but also a little trepidation, and that's what makes it fascinating for me. It's like opening a door onto a different world.

So my attention was totally focused on Sam, my hearing heightened to the sound and the level of her voice as she spoke, with full eye contact at all times. I asked her what I could do to help. She looked at her father, father looked at mother, and mother looked back at daughter. And then finally, father said, 'Tell him.'

I could see now that I was dealing with a strange family. I could see that they were reticent, each waiting for the other to speak. But I still needed to know what the issues were, and who was going to let me into this charged situation. It was eventually the father who eventually explained the full history. It was about a certain word, which it seemed was a trigger for Samantha to break down. That is, whenever a particular word was mentioned, Sam would have an emotional meltdown. Father was very careful not to say the word, which heightened the tension all round, of course – not least in me. But as I had to explain to them quite purposefully several times, I really needed to know what that certain word was if I was to understand how debilitating it was in the girl's life, and if I was to have any hope of helping her come to terms with it. Slowly it emerged that the word that caused all the difficulty would not be very debilitating for the majority of the year, but would become a real problem in December.

I started the hypnosis session and managed to successfully regress her back to an incident that happened in early childhood at a Christmas party. I discovered Sam was left sitting alone at a party while her parents went shopping. Goodness knows what the hosts were up to but nobody spoke or played with the little child during the whole party, and this had caused a chain of associations that had damaged her psychologically. Consequently, each year since, Sam had experienced a severe aversion to the word 'Christmas'. All the emotions of that day, recorded at the intense levels that children invest in the world around them, would be triggered by the word. Remember what it was like to be a child, when a lost toy could be as emotionally charged as a lost friend, causing paroxysms of tears and anguish. When triggered, Samantha would find herself back in the chaos of that room, abandoned by her mum and dad, not knowing if they would ever return. And so, during the festive season, when most kids are buzzing with excitement, and even at other times of the year, if Christmas was ever mentioned, she would get very upset and sob her heart out.

I was sure that I had managed to completely remove this seasonal aversion and, upon waking her, I asked how she felt and if she would allow me to say the 'C' word. Once again, she looked at father, father looked at mother, and mother looked at daughter, as I sat patiently waiting and wondering just what the outcome would be. Then father said, 'Tell him to say the word.'

Sam then looked at her father and said, 'Are you sure?'

Honestly, I was crawling up the walls by now, desperate to

scream bloody 'Christmas' at the top of my voice. But still the question bounced about the room. Father then finally looked at mother who at last said, 'Tell him to say the word.'

At this point I was baffled yet still needed to stay focussed. I really wanted Sam herself to ask me to say the blasted word as a sign of a new confidence and acceptance. Then, she did. Sam actually asked me to say the word.

'Happy ... Christmas,' I blurted out, in perhaps not too professional a manner. But, nevertheless, it was out there. The room went quiet, just for a second, and Sam's top lip quivered, just for a moment, and she said, 'I think I am cured!'

Sexual Fantasies

I regularly receive clients that suffer from emotional problems related to sex and I treat the subject no differently than, let's say for example, claustrophobia. One particular client came to see me that had developed a problem that meant she was unable to reach orgasm during sex with her partner. 'Jane' had never had this problem before and sex was a very important part of her relationship with her boyfriend.

Jane was an attractive girl in her mid-forties. After a comprehensive talk about the mechanics of hypnosis, and a quite in-depth – and, I would have to say, frank – discussion on what makes her 'tick', so to speak, we agreed on a mutually agreed approach to solving her problem under hypnosis.

Once again, I think the reader needs to visualise this scenario to get the complete effect of what it is like to be a hard-working hypnotherapist. You can imagine it, I'm sure: the phone is off, you have adopted a comfortable posture, in a very comfortable chair, the headphones are on with relaxing music, all the conditions were good for lift-off.

I was just about to start the induction when Jane's eyes popped opened and she asked if she could possibly lie down on the floor. If that was what was needed to make her comfortable, I replied that it was fine with me. Her head was now just resting on a cushion and, after she loosened the belt on her extremely tight jeans, she was now lying at my feet, ready to start. Once in a trance state, I dealt with her deep emotional feelings around orgasm and worked precisely to the script that we had both agreed upon. So I was now, in effect, talking dirty to this beautiful lady, to arouse her deep desires and associated sexual fantasies. And all for the benefit of some other very lucky man, who may have been totally unaware of all my labours. Mission complete, I now had to await feedback on the results.

Approximately two weeks later I received an email with a healthy thumbs up from Jane.

Peeping Tom

I will name my next client 'Neil', a tall, thinly built, rather reserved twenty-four-year old man. Neil had come to see me with a condition called 'shy bladder'. The condition is not uncommon and I had treated three similar clients previously. Neil had a psychological block which prevented him from going to the toilet 'for a wee' in public and he had to plan his day accordingly as to when he would take fluids. Whenever he was in a public toilet and looking to empty his bladder, he would simply freeze if another customer entered and be forced to make a quick exit. Even when out socially, he would have to basically plan ahead for every 'piddling' eventuality. Just imagine how terrible a problem this must be.

After explaining the process and preparing him for therapy, it transpired he was very susceptible to hypnosis and he allowed me easily into his subconscious. On this occasion, I used regression therapy to try and find out how and why this started, as Neil did not consciously know any reasons for his problem, and it had been this way for many years. He had got used to it, as humans are creatures of habit, and we have the ability to adapt and adjust to what is needed.

During the regression, I escorted him deep within his memory, back in time to his former years, back to being seven years old. I was very fortunate as I uncovered a memory that he had long forgotten, a memory of him in a public toilet on his own, when a man – likely a paedophile – blatantly watched him urinate. This negative memory was suppressed and long forgotten on a conscious level, but was the root cause of his problem. I managed to remove these negative memories then remove the link between the past and the present, before finally giving him positive suggestions to enable him to enter public toilets, without fear, like any other man.

Upon waking him, and after a glass of water and a final talk, I escorted him out of my office, instructing him to follow. 'Where are we going?' he asked. 'To the toilet,' I replied, 'for a pee.' He followed me in – I am sure apprehensively – but we stood side by side at the urinal in a public toilet, and we both emptied our bladders!

My Mind is a Living Hell

A year previously, I had dealt with a client that was not only claustrophobic but also agoraphobic. This condition had prevented this particular elderly client from leaving her home; she had been trapped there for almost thirty years! Her daughter had escorted her to my office and, by using the stairs and not the lift – and with a lot of cajoling – they had made their way up to see me. I was shocked to hear that the journey that day was one of only a handful of times she had left her home in many, many years. I knew just how important this session was to her.

My client desperately believed in me and I was, as always, going to give her my 100 per cent best. She was, luckily, very, very susceptible, and within the hour we were ready to put our session result into practise.

I took her by the arm and escorted her to the nearest lift. I called the lift and it arrived in seconds. 'Are you ready?' I asked. She nodded and, holding her hand, we both entered. I instructed her to press the button for the ground floor and, with a shaking hand, she slowly did. By the time we reached the ground floor, the smile on her face was of pure pleasure. It doesn't end there, though; I walked her out of the lobby and into the sunshine where she took my hand again – and we danced in the street! She was shouting to the pedestrians in the street, 'I am free, I am free!' It must have looked comical, but this was seriously a very important moment in this lady's life. After big hugs, and more big hugs, the lady departed with her daughter, big smiles on everyone's faces, including mine.

Psychological phobias are very, very common and removing them is a big part of my remit. The majority of issues that people suffer with develop at an early stage in life, usually during early childhood and that is why it is very important as parents to raise your children carefully. Young minds are extremely delicate and easily impressionable. Get it wrong and it could lead to serious emotional problems later in adult life. Sadly, this aspect of psychological parenting is absent in many cultures and societies and we are left to pick up the pieces. I think at this stage of the book it is appropriate to state that if you are struggling with an issue, please do not suffer in silence, GET HELP!

Cockroaches

I will now give you an example that I regularly tell to my clients seeking help to remove deep-seated phobias.

In 2012, I was treating a gentleman for a severe phobia of cockroaches. He was a level-headed man and I made sure that he already knew that a tiny insect, no matter how scary it looked, could not possibly harm him. However, this rational information had only entered the logical side of his brain, the other irrational hemisphere of the brain gave him tremors just thinking of them. It is interesting to note here that, in my experience, this type of phobia can be transmitted from one person to another.

Picture in your mind a young child whose whole world revolves around his or her family, with the centre of this intimate world as the mother. It's the summer months, and mum, who is also terrified of the cursed 'roaches' sees one on the kitchen floor and enters a state of complete meltdown. The child then observes this intensely dramatic situation and the fear generated by the insect. The mind, acting like a recorder, receives that the tiny cockroach is so dangerous that it is solely responsible for causing their mother's emotional breakdown and deeply retains this powerful negative experience. And so the seed is sown, into the next generation. You can see here why I want to stress the importance of raising children, not just by supplying a physically safe environment, but by also providing a mentally stable one, too.

So, back to my client, who was also terrified of cockroaches, though transference from a parent, in this case, had not been the cause of the manifestation. I worked this out early in our consultation. So, for my peace of mind, I needed now to get to his particular root cause.

He was a good subject for hypnosis and I successfully managed to guide him into a deep trance state, from where I used my 'magical' tool of regression therapy. After the deep induction, I took him back in time, way back to his earliest childhood memories. It transpired that during our hypnotic journey back, he discovered a memory lost with the passages of time. While playing with his older brother in the garden at the age of five, his brother had thrown a cockroach at him which had lodged in his shirt and dropped inside. The damned wriggling thing was trapped next to his skin and he panicked for several desperate minutes, trying to get it away from him, only to find bits of its mangled squirming body and its blood smeared across his chest. Ugh! And, all the while, his older brother was taunting him for being a sissy.

This was the trigger, a memory suppressed, buried inside him. A horrible memory linking disgust, his personal space violated and ridicule from someone close to him. Now knowing the root of the problem, I was then able to deal with the phobia and lay it to rest, and with additional suggestive therapy the client made a full recovery.

Having now given you a detailed example of how easily the mind can be scared, I will now tell you about the kind of case that makes my work rewarding beyond words can tell.

A Bird in Hand or in the Face

I had the pleasure in the autumn months of 2013 of removing an intense phobia of birds, in particular pigeons, from a ten-year-old girl, that I shall name 'Jacey', which had developed five years earlier, while Jacey was celebrating her fifth birthday with friends and family. A clown was employed to entertain the children, and during the entertainment the clown produced a pigeon from out of his sleeve, and as it emerged it flew hard and fast straight into young Jacey's face. It was such a shock to the system that it took the parents quite a while to calm her down. And from that day, Jacey developed an intense fear of all birds, and especially pigeons, as you can imagine.

This fear grew stronger and to such a point that whenever she went out of her home, her subconscious 'pigeon radar' was activated. A trip out to the city became impossible due to this fear. Jacey, now ten, came to see me with her parents. She was a lovely young girl and after a one hour session I managed to completely remove all traces of the negative emotion and fear. A few days later I heard via social media that she was a totally different person and had already travelled into the city. I was also thanked not only by her parents but by her uncles and aunts as well. It was a good result, but it is worth noting that Jacey had previously suffered five years of unnecessary hell before she was brought to see me.

Mr Bates, Can I *Smoke* but Not Smoke?

Results with hypnotherapy differ with each client. For example, if I stopped a smoker from smoking all tobacco products today, he or she may definitely state that they'll never smoke again. Yet, a different client, although making the same statement – and apparently just as sincere – may start smoking again the very next day.

Every human is unique. But, statistically, I have a very good track record, particularly with this therapy, and I can boast the fact, as results speak for themselves. But of all the help I give using hypnosis, smoking cessation therapy, I find, is one of the easiest, and the results are instantly obvious compared with, for example, weight loss or even fear of flying.

I practise therapy in many countries and in the late nineties, about to travel to another country by air, I was stopped at immigration. The officer took me to one side and said, 'Mr Bates, I have an appointment to see you this week for smoking cessation but I have a slight problem.' He continued, 'I smoke and I *smoke* if you understand? Will it still be ok for me to *smoke* and not to smoke?'

It was a good job I knew where he was coming from or I would have been completely lost, and for the innocent reader that is now lost, I will explain. He meant he smoked cannabis and wanted to continue smoking his 'wacky backy' but not cigarettes.

Believe it or not this is a very common question that I am asked, which suggests that the smoking of cannabis is very widespread.

Coca-Cola or Water

In 2013, I was conducting a group weight loss session. It was attended by thirty-five clients and the session is similar to weight watchers or slimmer's world but with one big difference. Rather than talking about eating habits, etc., I was hypnotically embedding into their subconscious very important suggestions to retrain their minds to reduce the sugar content, portion sizes and carb content of their diet, and to also place motivations for exercise, along with other lifestyle changes that would help make a difference.

One of my male clients was doing everything wrong imaginable, and I mean everything. He was seriously obese and clinically needed to lose weight. What stood out with this chap and separated him from everybody else was that, importantly, he did not drink any water, only Coca-Cola. And he drank two large bottles of it every day – in total, four litres – and had done so for many years! There are 240 grams of sugar in each two litre bottle of Coca-Cola. This alone would cause serious health problems for any person in due time.

During this particular group session, I included something just for him, to stress the need to switch away from high calorie drinks.

After the session ended I instructed, as always in this type of therapy, that all the clients that received a positive result should attend the following month in order to reinforce the suggestions, as this intensifies the whole process. The same man attended a month later and, upon asking him how he was doing, he replied, 'Terrible! Not lost any weight yet. But since I attended the last session, I bloody hate Coke!'

Well, okay, he did not lose weight that month, but his mind was retrained to hate Coca-Cola, and he was now drinking water. This in my eyes was a massive result, a result that could possibly save his life.

Rape

I received a request for help from a young lady that, at the time, I did not know very well. She informed me that she had been raped. (She has insisted that I use her real name in covering this story. I asked her to reconsider, so that I could conceal her identity, but she wants the world to know her real identity, as she has nothing at all to be ashamed of, and says that if she can help just one victim, then it is all worthwhile.)

Erica sought help in April 2003 after watching one of my shows at a local hotel, where she was a barmaid, but only after she could muster up the courage to ask. Erica had been suffering in silence and the emotional pressure had built up to such a degree that it was affecting all aspects of her life. Not only had she been sexually assaulted but, since the attack, her problems had continued. After the rape, and in the due course of time, she had had other relationships, but they were also subject to other forms of physical, emotional and sexual abuse. She had just set out on another relationship that she really hoped would be a wholesome and loving one, but she was rightly still deeply unsettled and confused by the direction that her life had taken, and she was silently crying out for help

We arranged a mutual time to meet and I am very happy to report that there was a successful outcome to the session that allowed Erica to face life again. Erica had already met the man of her dreams, Peter, and they were engaged to be married. She was now mentally ready to start living her life to the full.

Shortly afterwards, I received a very touching poem from Erica that described her emotions during the session. I have included this poem below (see next page).

Erica and Peter's relationship blossomed and on 7 July 2007 they tied the knot and were happily married, and they are now blessed with two beautiful children. And the icing on the cake for me was that due to Erica not having a father around to give her away at her wedding, I was asked to walk her down the aisle and into a fairy-tale ending!

Your voice sounds just like chocolate tastes,
I feel myself wanting to listen closer,
To listen more carefully, I want to hear more.
I close my eyes and concentrate on what you are saying,
Focusing my mind solely on your voice,
I do not want to listen to, or think about anything else.
Nothing enters my mind but the sound of your voice.
Soothing. Calming and tranquil.
I want to concentrate on what you are saying,
But all I can hear is your voice,
I am not aware of the words I am hearing,
Just the lull that I feel as a result.
I feel as though I am floating,
So serene, so relaxed and so focused,
Focused upon nothing but the inflection of your voice.
I never want this feeling to end,
I feel so calm, so at peace with the world.

Then suddenly it is over.
The spell is broken.
You voice is silent.

I smile; the serenity is still here,
I feel calm, peaceful and relaxed.
I have no memory of the words that were spoken,
Just the feeling of hope you instilled in my mind.
A spark left to burn; a consequence of hypnosis.

A poem by Erica Case, A Consequence of Hypnosis

13. Lady in Red

Gaining a client's trust during hypnotherapy is always necessary for a successful outcome of psychological therapy. So, no matter what clients' issues I have to deal with, I always conduct myself in a most professional manner, part of which is to not judge people by how they present themselves, which can be sometimes very hard not to do. I try never to be surprised by the styles that present themselves for therapy, but I am constantly surprised by the layers and depths that each of us carry within us, layers of which we are mostly totally unaware. But there are times of course when I am shaken, if not stirred, which again adds a certain something, a certain spice, to the working day.

There was one lady that did sneak under the radar and get me rather rattled. Let's call her 'Jane'. Jane booked to see me for an afternoon appointment for smoking cessation, and she duly arrived on time. When I opened the door to receive her I was bowled over by the impact of this very attractive girl. I am all too human, as you may have already worked out, and I reacted by instinct rather than training. She smiled; my instant very 'human' and 'instinctive' assessment must have been written all over my face.

She arrived at my consulting room dressed in a short and very pretty cherry red dress, red high heeled shoes, earrings and necklace, carrying a red Prada handbag – all perfectly matching this rich, blood-red shade, which must have had a hell of an impact on the street; it certainly did at close quarters. In fact, she looked like she was going to a party – and a very grand party at that – rather than attending therapy, which is, of course, meant to be a 'working' situation. I quickly gathered my composure and I'm sure I calmly introduced myself, welcomed her into my office and directed her to the comfortable therapy chair. Now, this therapy chair suddenly, and for the first time, presented itself to me as a real problem as the dress material was not only emphasising every shape and movement, but there was very little of it anywhere, particularly in the lower region. Although there wasn't a great deal in the bodice part either. I was, in fact, wrong to call it a dress really as it was, for all the world, more like a very stylish and 'wide-ish' sort of belt.

Now I was worried for a moment, but Jane was not the slightest bit uncomfortable. As she sat down she lifted both of her legs up and over and this very short dress rode right up her legs, so much so that I noticed that the underwear matched the whole outfit perfectly.

I am certainly no prude but I was thrown completely off track as my mind raced to come to terms with what had just happened. I treated this pretty client no different to any other but, as I knew I was compromised, I focused totally on trying to hold eye-to-eye contact throughout our dialogue. As I mentioned, the appearance of a client is an important part of the profile that I build up of the person before me. And, always before I start any therapy, I discuss the client's background. I think of this, as I also explain it to them, as having in my mind a mental jigsaw puzzle, with their name on each piece. Once all the pieces are joined together I am ready to start the session.

She explained to me that outwardly her life seemed complete and that she had everything money could buy: the perfect house, cars and all the obvious trappings of success. However, deep down she was still unsatisfied, which was why she thought she was smoking so many cigarettes. She went on further to explain that she felt her husband, although perfect in lots of ways as a provider, was not providing sufficient attention in the bedroom department. This was the reason she was now smoking, out of boredom, and that this had now got out of hand and needed to stop. Many people smoke for these reasons, she was right. Often, it is a distraction mechanism, and this really did need to change, as we all know the damage it can cause.

Jane also mentioned as we chatted that she had seen me on television, some time earlier. I felt that, in her mind, she saw me as a celebrity rather than a therapist and, with the wonderful benefit of hindsight, having had time to digest and analyse what happened, I believe she came to see me more out of a lustful fantasy than to actually give up smoking. 'Celebrity' is a very glamorous, but two-dimensional, image; and it is a contrived image at that. Often, as we know from the newspapers and the scandal sheets, this image has little to do with the real person behind the 'mask' of fame.

Subconsciously, this lovely lady had fallen for the tinsel. She would 'know' consciously that this was a very short-sighted level of attraction, and maybe she didn't care or didn't see, I don't know. And, maybe, that was why she offered a similar show-stopping eye-candy version of a smoking cessation hypnosis session to me. Looking back, I am still glad that nothing happened between us that day. And, to my credit, I can even say that, as she sat down in that wonderfully inappropriate and lustful way, my professional 'self' gave her a towel to place over her lap, to *save her dignity*; it was, by the way, beyond any saving, but at least it allowed me to concentrate and focus on my work.

And, as you've probably guessed already, the smoking cessation never worked.

14. Hunt the Gunman

During the early period of learning my trade, and well before I had even thought of helping people with their psychological issues, I got myself involved with a very interesting and rather scary situation. This was back home in the same town that I first saw the light of day – Wallasey, Wirral, UK.

The episode happened while I was performing a comedy show in a small social club. I was approached by two rather anxious ladies named Gillian and Beverly. When I had some time after the show, we sat down and they explained that they both worked at a local bank and that a week earlier they had been held up at gunpoint. The robbers had got away with a substantial amount of money. They then went on to explain that at one point a gun was pointed at Gillian's stomach and another aimed at a colleague's head. This had obviously been such a terrifying experience that they had suffered, as both of them were experiencing the effects of trauma, with not only the jumpiness, anxiety and physical tension aspects that one might expect from the terrible stress they had endured, but both were also suffering from an inability to sleep and a general nervousness and failure to relax in simple, everyday situations. What concerned them both was that they had also suffered amnesia around the details and events of that fateful day. Thereby, they were unable to supply the police with any positive information.

I could see that the girls were still really suffering from this awful experience so I offered to try and help them. We discussed the event and by getting a clearer picture I began explaining that there was a possibility that hypnosis may be able to help them. Both ladies felt that this was a good way forward and so a date was agreed for me to meet them at their home.

By virtue of the fact that the meeting was to be held a couple of evenings later, I had the opportunity to thoroughly think things through and research what method would be best able to approach the therapy. The ladies' welfare and their recovery had to be my paramount concern. However, beyond that, if I could help recover any information that might help the police, this would be considered a bonus. Both Gillian and Beverly proved to be excellent subjects for hypnosis. Working with each lady separately, they each went into a deep trance state.

To increase the effect of the recall they would experience, I used a technique called regression therapy. Regression therapy involves using the subconscious mind to replay events that have happened in the past, to recall things that the conscious mind has disavowed and forgotten. I worked hard to ensure that it was to be without any negative emotions, stress or panic. It would be just like watching a movie, but in slow motion. Unless you have experienced this type of therapy, it is hard to imagine just how effective it can be. But if the scenes are strongly imagined in this way, and the client can disengage and create the emotional 'distance' necessary, it can reduce a great deal of the effects of fear, and it is often used in cases of trauma and strong aversions.

In this case, it worked amazingly well with both the trauma and the amnesia that it had inflicted, and more information about the robbery was revealed. The information was useful in assisting the police in their bid to catch the robbers. One piece of the forgotten jigsaw that returned was that one of the raiders had taken off a glove at a certain point in the robbery, so he could get a better grip on a handle to get into a cupboard. Now, this information meant that the police were enabled to get fingerprints in an area that had previously been thought of no concern. This valuable supressed information was considered unimportant at the time. Survival and safety would have been the ladies' prime consideration with guns pointing at heads and threats flying in their direction. But the mind, although focused elsewhere, nevertheless is still noticing all this 'irrelevant' information. And, what is more, recording it in detail. The word 'forgotten' can be a very loaded word for me when I work with people, and it has a whole range of different meanings in the field of hypnosis.

The police were satisfied with the help that we were able to give them, but the work with the two girls continued beyond that. We worked then to release some of the thoughts from the robbery that had hit them particularly hard and left the deepest negative impressions. I also continued giving both of them strategies for directed 'forgetting', with positive images and suggestions and reinforcement to help each of them with the particular parts of the incident that had inflicted their post-traumatic stress disorder (PTSD). Slowly but surely, their bodies relaxed more, the fears faded and their nightmares subsided. Fairly soon they returned back to work and to the regular hurly-burly of Wirral life.

It was great to have helped these very plucky ladies. They were both really good to work with and seemed to take naturally to this 'unique' type of work, like ducks to water, and they were both genuinely appreciative of my assistance, which is always lovely to hear. But when the local newspaper was delivered two days later, to my horror I saw my picture. The story of what happened was front page news!

Sometimes, though thankfully not in this case, publicity associated with a crime or high profile 'drama' like this can put ordinary folk off the whole idea of hypnosis all together. They separate it from themselves and the everyday problems for which it is also really successful. As we have shown, 'the mind' has illogical associations and they just do not want to link in any way to such situations. Most people see through this and can hopefully work out that those same skills could help them to redirect the smaller, but still stifling and restricting, 'hang-ups' that we all can suffer from, from time to time – sometimes for many years – until we actively 'do' something about it.

I had no idea the press would be involved, and for some time later I was fearful for my safety. I have included a copy of the front page story from the newspaper.

Front page news, featuring the author

15. Buried Alive

This story involves another club on the fringes of a nightlife that caters to those who enjoy the kind of good time that stretches comfort zones. And in this case, it certainly coaxed me way, way beyond mine.

This time I was performing at a venue named Evergreens in Stoke-on-Trent, Staffordshire, UK. It was a 'fun' venue, very popular, and a great place to perform. This successful venue was run by two good friends of mine, Liverpudlians Ronnie & Jackie James, and this venue operated an 'anything and everything goes' policy.

While attending a production / show development meeting I was asked if I would allow myself to be buried in a coffin, six feet deep, for one day, to help raise money for Barnardo's, a well known UK children's charity. And, even more surprising to me, looking back, is that I agreed.

Evergreens was such an outrageous place. Once I was a witness to an outrageous dinner party. A table was set out in silver service style with napkins and candelabras while three men and one woman, all in immaculate evening dress, sat down to dine – but with a big difference. Firstly, the table was located on the stage, in view for all the audience to see, and, secondly, the menu was distinctly limited – the *special* of the day was Pedigree Chum dog food and Kitty Cat! The competition winner would be the first to finish and, yes, surprisingly, they all ate everything that was put before them.

But, as with all these things, sometimes things did not go like clockwork. Of course, this is where the excitement enters. It is the 'will they won't they?' aspect of these episodes that makes them fascinating. And it's the ones that go wrong – thankfully, not terribly wrong – that keep us glued to our seats. As a regular entertainer at this extreme entertainment place, I remember one particular event when I witnessed a charity fundraiser that really was not thought through properly by the 'escapologist', who really should have been prosecuted under the Trade Descriptions Act.

The poor guy was padlocked in a straitjacket and placed in a large barrel of water with a sealed lid on top, and the objective was to escape within one minute. He must have had the heart of a lion as he really believed he could do this trick, but he had not even tried it before! Not only did he not escape but after a few very tense moments the big barrel had to be kicked over and the wannabe Houdini had to be resuscitated! Such was the nature of this crazy entertainment venue that the customer, and in this case also the artist himself, really never knew what would hit them next? A lot of cold water in this case.

So my burial was set to take place on a Monday, a public bank holiday, and one of the most popular bank holidays of the British summer, 28 August 1989, at high noon. I know I am making this sound dramatic, but please remember, reader, that from my perspective, it really was.

We were expecting big crowds. I had invited my younger brother, John, to help me with this one – this way, I knew he would attend at least the first one of my funerals. He and I had set in place plans that would ensure that I would survive the claustrophobic coffin that would be my temporary resting place for the designated time underground. Get it wrong and the final curtain would come down for sure. Even my dear mother, who normally isn't fazed by my antics, was concerned by this one and, thank goodness, she refused to come, otherwise it would have been too real – for her and me.

And, I must admit, that with the lead up to my burial, I did have second thoughts, and then third and fourth thoughts as well, and all of them of backing down. But **NO**, in the entertainment business, the show goes on – and, as a true professional, I was not about to let down my faithful fans, after all, they had turned up for my funeral. And I suppose it wouldn't have been the first time that I had died on stage anyway.

At exactly midday, the lid was sealed on the coffin and I was lowered into the cold bosom of the earth. A eulogy was read out by my friend, DJ Jacko, dressed as a vicar and I suppose that it was only then that it really hit me what was happening.

I started to panic and my life flashed in front of me in what seemed like seconds. It suddenly became very, very real. I really struggled. Imagine this with me for a moment; the worst part of the whole experience was the silence and the sudden loneliness, I was on my own, far from the crowds and the fun and the noise of life. As far as I was concerned, I was listening to the sound of the soil being shovelled onto the coffin lid by the gravediggers. Not many folk would ever experience the heavy thump of this horrific sound from underneath the soil, as I was. What must it be like for those poor souls who come round at this stage for real, not dead but in exactly the same situation as me, but without the lifelines I had the courtesy of. And which my life was now totally depending upon. I knew

John and I had designed them well, but I began worrying if we had designed them well enough.

I lay there, just listening, until the muffled sound slowly disappeared. I was completely on my own, more than I had ever been in any situation in my life, hemmed in, in pure serene silence. Once settled, I could control the compressed, fresh, clean air that was supplied to me by a compressor via a pipe on the surface, diligently operated by John. I hope he's not drinking too many toasts to 'absent friends', I thought. This was essential for survival as all that soil, if not the box itself, was airtight, and once the air that you breathe inside the coffin expires, then, in effect, you are breathing pure carbon dioxide, which is a killer.

I even had a headstone and flowers placed on my grave to add insult to injury, but all this seemed a 'great idea' in the initial planning stages. I had to make myself relax, control my breathing and make myself keep calm. By now, the very large gathering of people there to witness my burial, whether for curiosity or for morbid reasons, or to just dance on my grave, I didn't know, had retired for liquid refreshments. I will give you one guess only to who was left mourning at my graveside. Throughout the ordeal, sitting and whimpering at the grave, was my faithful friend, Trixie, my dog!

If you were to lock your wife and your dog in the boot of your car for one whole hour, when you opened the boot who do you think would be excited and really glad to see you? Exactly, such is the love of your dog.

So this is what being buried forever feels like, I thought, in the material way of course. As, in the realms of physics, energy cannot be destroyed, and I like to believe our 'essence', our spirit, our consciousness, or whatever you may want to call it, is transported elsewhere after physical death. It would be such a waste, in my opinion, that when our physical body is finished with all life's experiences, its emotions, trials and tribulations, that they are simply dissolved away.

Alone now for six hours. What shall I do, I thought. During my restful, though immobile and claustrophobic, time in the coffin, I had a telephone link to BBC Radio Staffordshire, and they were broadcasting live my progress on the hourly news, thus creating even more public interest. But, more importantly, we were raising money – thanks to the great British public, as well as my fans and audience, and no doubt the odd few voyeurs – which, of course, was the very reason for me doing such a bizarre fundraiser!

Time initially passed rather quickly and I used a deep meditation, very similar to a sort of hypnotic trance – a self-inflicted human hibernation state of mind – to allow the time to pass. Before long, my walkie-talkie radio crackled into life. It was a female voice, a voice that I didn't recognise, and the conversation that followed could not possibly be printed here. This was apparently a random stranger who had picked up the radio and was talking in a very flirtatious manner to me, and then it stopped as abruptly as it started. After the burial had ended, and while driving home, I asked John who this person might have been but he had no idea who I was talking about. Thankfully, the next time the walkie-talkie radio crackled, it was to inform me that a massive crowd was gathering around my graveside in anticipation of my resurrection.

Believe it or not, I managed to change clothes in the coffin, in preparation for the resurrection. I felt like a contortionist, trying to undress and dress, and I was sure that I had my pants on the wrong way round, but that was all to be expected. I had organised it so that when the coffin lid was removed, I was sporting a creepy Halloween skull and skeletal costume, which gave the spectators quite a shock, particularly the younger children that had managed to crawl between their parents' legs for a graveside view.

It was a really, really strange experience as the gravediggers were getting closer to my coffin. Slowly, their sounds brought life back from the serene silence, first a gentle soft shuffle, and then dull thuds as the spades came nearer and nearer. This was followed by a building of the muffled sounds of the curious who crowded around the grave – my grave. Then, growing from this, the almost audible human conversations and buzz of those closest to the graveside. And as the last pieces of earth were brushed off the coffin lid, I was really now so excited that I nearly shouted back to them. I had actually done it and I was still alive to tell the tale – and to write about it. And, unknown to me at the time, but very importantly to give this madcap stunt a serious point, a lot of money was raised by my crazy endeavours for this very worthy charity. As the 'vicar' read passages from the Bible, the coffin lid was prized open and, to the sound of Michael Jackson's 'Thriller', I lurched out to a wonderful cheer from the very inebriated parish mourners. The time was now 6.00 p.m. I was buried alive for exactly six hours; although, in the end, it felt like twenty to me in such pitch black confinement. And it was time now to attend the traditional 'wake'. My very own wake!

In towns and cities throughout England, in times gone by, they would often run out of places to bury people. So they would dig up coffins, take the bones to a bone-house, and reuse the grave. When reopening these coffins, 1 out of 25 were found to have scratch marks on the inside – they had been burying people alive. As you can imagine, this was a terrible fate to imagine for your loved ones or oneself. So to try to prevent this happening they would sometimes tie a string on the wrist of the corpse, lead it through the coffin and up through the ground and to a bell. Someone would have to sit out in the graveyard all night – literally, 'the graveyard shift' – to listen for the bell. Thus, someone could be 'saved by the bell' or was considered a 'dead ringer'.

Would I do it again? The answer should be no but, dear reader, being a sucker for a good cause the answer is yes, and I did do it again. I did not think it at the time but I would repeat this ludicrously dangerous and frightening stunt again for another worthy charity in Malta in 2002. And it would be televised this time, and on a much grander scale.

There was an extremely sad ending to working at this wonderful venue, Evergreens. The original management team, Liverpudlians Ronnie and Jackie, left that club to return to work in a new venue in Paradise Street, Liverpool. After a short while at their new premises, an intruder stayed hidden in the bar after closing time, intending to steal the contents from the safe, and Ronnie discovered him. Knowing Ronnie as I did, this would not have been acceptable, and Ronnie paid with his life, stabbed sixteen times. A distraught Jackie was to discover his blood-soaked body shortly afterwards. The murderer was eventually apprehended by the diligent work of Merseyside police, convicted, and is now justly serving life imprisonment.

Malta had now become almost my second home with very frequent working visits, which included television appearances, comedy shows and personal therapy sessions. After my initial corporate show on the lovely island of Gozo, Marcette, my Maltese manager, initiated discussions on how to raise awareness and funds for Razzett tal–Hbiberija, a facility for disabled people, and it was agreed that I would undertake once again my 'being buried alive in a coffin' stunt. I knew I *could* do it, due to my past exploits from many years back in England. But there are always risks attached to this sort of activity. This time, though, it would be conducted on a much more majestic scale, and so the date was set. Marcette rapidly put in place everything that I requested, in a most professional manner, assisted by her brother, Tonio, who ensured that the safety and logistics were in place. *Xarabank*, a very popular TV programme, covered the event but other Maltese channels, including the news media network, also ran the story.

Roadside billboard for live TV show, Malta

I have a big fan base in Malta and a lot of my fans gathered to witness the committal as I was buried very deep in the grounds at Razzett tal–Hbiberija in Marsascala. Unlike my previous 'pauper's burial', this time I had the dignity of a granite engraved headstone and a full island nation of mourners! But I need not have worried – this time I had full back-up on site, with all the emergency services present, including the fire service, doctors, National Guard and, of course, the TV and press.

I was exhumed in the evening, as was the plan, and again, like back at the first burial in England, all the 'mourners' had returned to witness my resurrection. And as I was received from the cold bosom of 'mother earth', I received lots of attention from the doctors checking my stats – hydration levels, pulse, etc. My first answer to the live TV news presenter was, 'I now know what it feels like when someone has walked on your grave!'

After reading this story you may be asking yourself, is Alan Bates going to be buried or *cremated* when he eventually passes away?

Simple answer, actually, I am going to be cremated! Just for a change.

The resurrection, author exhumed from the grave in Malta

16. A Royal Confession

Early hours on 1 April 1992, I was awakened by an overseas telephone call. The call sounded particularly loud. My head was still spinning and dizzy from a really good party that evening. The line was rather poor and the voice on the other end said, 'Alan, its Crystal. I am calling from Brunei and I have an important gig for you.' My brain began then to engage as the excited voice continued. 'Alan, listen to me. The American singer and showman, MC Hammer, has let Princess Hamidah down on her fifteenth birthday party and they need a replacement act pretty quick. I put your name forward and they have accepted.' I was totally confused and Crystal needed answers right away. Luckily, my immediate answer was, 'Yes! Get the flight tickets booked.' Crystal was very excited. She thanked me and then allowed me to go back to sleep.

I awoke several hours later with the phone on my chest and a hangover. Strangely distorted thoughts of a dream about being invited to Brunei or some far distant place to perform for royalty filled my head. The dream felt so real but I started to doubt the whole thing after ringing friends and family and telling them about it. They all laughed and said, 'Alan, its April Fool's Day –

April Fool!' I let a couple of days pass but I still had this dream on my mind, and so I decided I needed to sort my head out. After half an hour searching my databases I found the telephone number for Crystal's mum in Manchester. I made a call and her mum confirmed that her daughter was employed by his Royal Highness, Prince Jefri Bolkiah, in Brunei, and that she worked as his personal DJ for private functions and as a companion for his young daughter, Princess Hamidah.

My heart was now pumping. If it was a dream it was a really perceptive one; after all, I could not have known the details that Crystal's mum had given me. I had no contact number in Brunei and I could not even remember the date of the party. But, importantly, I did remember giving her my address.

On 4 April, I was once again awakened early by a courier service wanting a signature for a small package. As I opened the envelope, to my amazement, air tickets fell out and I watched this dream become a reality in front of me. There it was, clear as day, and in black and white – and a few other colours – a return ticket with Singapore Airlines, *'first class'*. I was now completely awake, my hands were shaking, and I had to read the information on the tickets three times before it sunk in. I was going out to Brunei on 24 April 1992, and returning on the 27th to perform a hypnosis show for the Brunei royal family, who were then, I believe, the richest family in the world.

Really excited, I called my parents and family to tell them my good news. They were thrilled for me as this was a one-off lifetime experience and I was determined to enjoy every second. I received another call from Crystal, instructing me that I was not to tell anybody apart from my immediate family, for security reasons.

Stage fright is not something I suffered from but the days leading up to my departure were anxious ones for me. I would walk up and down the hallway as if treading the boards backstage before a show, wondering what to expect from the Far East, and which routines would I perform that would be in keeping for a royal performance. Who would attend the show and what type of young lady would the Princess turn out to be?

Departure day finally arrived. I arrived at Manchester airport, departing on schedule and, upon check-in with Singapore Airlines, I was very impressed by their high standards. I was presented with an invitation to the VIP lounge where airline staff attended to my every need. I was not used to first class at airports. Up until then, all my flights were economy. I boarded the aircraft and was offered champagne. Wonderful! I was certainly going to enjoy this one. The flight purser introduced himself and addressed me as 'Mr Alan'. He informed me that if there was anything I required, all I needed to do was to ask. I had a cheesy grin from ear to ear.

International Comedy Festival, Malaysia, 2015

It was a very long flight indeed, the longest I had ever undertaken. I was to arrive at the airport early evening so I spent my time watching several movies and drinking copious amounts of champagne and the best Scotch whisky. I started to feel the effects. Each time my glass ran dry the flight attendant was there to fill it back up again —what a life! I managed to get a little sleep and before I knew it we were on our final approach into Lapangan Terbang Antarabangsa airport, Brunei. I was instructed not to tell anybody my business in Brunei, not even the customs or immigration officials, should I be questioned. I was rather concerned by this as, if I were to get asked, what on earth would I say?

I checked through immigration without a hitch but at the carousal I waited for my baggage and, to my disappointment, it wasn't there. I was now the only passenger left standing at the carousal with several customs officers watching me. I was now concerned and nervous. I approached them and explained about my missing suitcase and a tall officer in an immaculate uniform asked me about the one case that had been revolving for the last ten minutes. I turned and looked and, to my horror, it was my case,

Welcome to India initiation; in the country with UTV World Movies plus a Mumbai Theatre tour

and it had been there all the time! I was instructed to open it and I thought that's it, what on earth do I say now? How am I going to explain away my stage props consisting of a six foot long plastic boa constrictor snake, spiders, a skull and other strange stage props? The officer was not perturbed and beckoned me through.

The small airport was now completely devoid of passengers and, fortunately, I cleared customs without a further hitch. I towed my suitcase on its rear wheels out of the terminal building and to my further horror there was not one person outside, not a single car or even a taxi. I waited for a further ten minutes in complete darkness in a high temperature – no streetlights, no contact telephone number. Just silence.

I became rather concerned, I did not know who was to meet me or where I was to stay, and considering I was instructed to keep quiet about my purpose of visitation, I really didn't know what on earth to do! I was jet lagged, tired and still half drunk on the complimentary delights when I decided to return back into the terminal building and get someone to call me a taxi.

I arrived at the Sheraton Utama Hotel in Bandar Seri Begawan and to my total surprise I already had a reservation, and several messages were awaiting me from Crystal. The instructions were to freshen up (sober up!) and meet for dinner at nine-thirty. The hotel was of a good standard and later I was to discover that the Brunei people were generally extremely humble, sincere, honest and very friendly. Apart from their mother language, Malay, they also all spoke very good English. I made my dinner appointment on time and was greeted by Crystal with a big friendly hug. We had a lot of catching up to do and I had many, many questions to be answered. Crystal had come a long way from a well-known nightclub DJ in Manchester to becoming a royal servant and friend to the richest family on the planet!

Over dinner we got ourselves up to speed and all the rules were spelled out to me. I was to meet Princess Hamidah the following day. A party was being thrown to celebrate her birthday in the Princess's own nightclub, with one exception: no alcohol. This was the rule of the whole, strictly Muslim, country. It was explained that the nightclub was built exactly to western standards with all the very latest equipment, and musically they were up to date though only a few kids attended her club.

It didn't take long for me to realise that 95 per cent of the hotel patrons were on the Sultan's payroll. This was big business and when you are dealing with the richest family in the world, that big contract could make you very wealthy. I met a vast array of characters during my short stay, including many salesmen tendering for contracts that ranged from helicopters to gold bath taps, all hoping to succeed with their business.

I retired to bed with my head filled with our dinner conversation, jet lagged and still buzzing from the whole experience. I was to be picked up early in the morning and driven to meet Princess Hamidah and so I needed to have all my wits about me. I was determined to enjoy every second of this royal experience in Brunei, my only regret is that I forgot to take a camera with me. Daybreak arrived and, after a hearty breakfast, Crystal came to meet me to escort me to the palace. In Brunei royal circles, all the palaces are referred to in 'house numbers'.

As we approached a sentry box, I was informed that the royal family were protected by their own army which was a detachment of British-trained Ghurkhas. Crystal, with her long blond hair and blue eyes, stood out a mile. She was a well-known face and was waved on through the casual checkpoint. My adrenaline was pumping now. I was just minutes away from meeting a real princess. To calm me down, Crystal said, 'Chill out, Alan, Princess Hamidah is really looking forward to meeting you as well.' We were now in the royal grounds. We drove past two long buildings on split-levels, which were Prince Jefri's garages, and my eyes popped out of my head when I saw the contents! Crystal informed me that I could enjoy a guided tour around the garages later – first we were to meet Princess Hamidah.

As we pulled up in the courtyard, we parked next to a brand new yellow Ferrari. I noticed a little electric golf buggy making its way up to join us. Crystal said, 'Here she is. This is the Princess and you're here to entertain her.' Wow, that was a good way to put it. I was not sure how I was going to play this one. Should I be calm and shy? Or do I act myself and be outgoing and friendly? I quickly decided to be my cheeky self. Princess Hamidah pulled up alongside our car and, accompanying her, was her cousin Citi.

The Princess shyly got out of her buggy and came over to meet us. Crystal introduced me and with a nice smile I thanked her for inviting me to Brunei. The Princess in turn introduced me to her cousin, who was of a similar age. I could see both girls were interested in me, purely for the reason they did not get to meet boys – certainly not cheeky English ones with fair hair and blue eyes. I now felt so much at ease. Apart from her royal status, Hamidah was just a young pretty girl who wanted to know as much about me as I did her. We hit it off as the afternoon progressed and the Princess asked, 'Would you like to see our polo horses?' I replied, 'Sure thing,' and we drove around to the stables. Prince Jefri retained a full Argentinian polo team for whenever he felt in the mood.

The Princess then asked if I would like a ride. I replied, 'I would love to.' One of the Argentinian stablemen beckoned me to a horse, which I mounted without any fear. My younger days spent on a local farm in my home town would now come in handy. These horses were the best that money could buy. Once the Princess had mounted, we were off. We did a circuit of the stables and then it was back to the group. The Princess had a bodyguard who was present most of the time. He seemed to appear out of thin air and kept himself very much to himself. Looking back now, he was not the type of man you would want to get on the wrong side of – 'special forces', for sure. Once we finished riding, the Princess was much more relaxed in my company and I suggested we go to the club where I was to perform the following day, so that I could get a feel for the place. We made our way to the venue and, after closer examination, I was very surprised to find the club better equipped than most of the UK nightclubs in which I had worked as a professional DJ.

I was now starting to see the power and wealth of this family. Cheekily, I asked Princess Hamidah what birthday gifts she had received and she casually pulled down the neck of her sweatshirt and revealed a most beautiful diamond necklace. Then she tugged at her ears to highlight her matching earrings. I was told later that the set was bought in London for over one million pounds. I was then cheeky enough again to ask what else she had received and she took me by my arm to the courtyard and pointed to the bright yellow Ferrari, next to which we had parked earlier. We got into the car, the Princess in the driving seat, but she did not know how to drive, and the crazy thing is her feet would not reach the pedals.

The Princess then told me it was to add to her colour collection of Ferraris! As the afternoon progressed, I was becoming fed up addressing her as 'Princess Hamidah'. It seemed long and drawn out, and whilst we were in mid-conversation, I felt brave –and cheeky enough – to ask. I said quickly, 'Do you mind if I call you Hamidah.' She replied, 'I don't mind,' so from then on we were on first-name terms.

The sun had started to set and it was time for us to leave the palace. Crystal asked if I would like to visit the world famous

Water Village, the largest in the world, and watch the sunset. I was very keen to see as much of this lovely country as I possibly could in the short time available. The Water Village is a whole village built above the water line, supported by timber posts and built entirely of wood, with creaky passageways as the infrastructure.

We walked out onto the village and all the homes were open to see – little children were being bathed and put to bed, families preparing food. The residents were extremely friendly and I made a special effort to wave to all the kids and parents alike. The homes were very clean and tidy and I remember thinking at the time what a wonderful way of life – zero crime, no stress, and no major competition. Just a great and simple community spirit. Crystal told me that the Sultan had offered to build a whole new village on land but the residents refused as this had been their way of life for generations. The rumour was that when the Sultan married, he bought a television set for everybody that wanted one, so they could all watch the ceremony live. At this time, I would never have dreamed that one day I would be the first hypnotist on TV there and my show would be broadcast live from Kuala Lumpur throughout the whole region.

We arrived back at the hotel after a very fulfilling day and with just enough time to shower and dress for dinner. I was told that the British, American, Australian and European employees were told of my arrival and all wanted to dine with us. At the time, after sunset, everything stopped in Brunei. There are no cafés, restaurants, clubs or streetlights that I knew about, and it gets very dark. Upon arriving at the hotel restaurant, I was greeted by about twenty-five people. We sat around several tables and ordered local cuisine. It was such a shame there was no wine or alcohol to complement our excellent feast, only soft drinks. Our dinner conversation covered many topics, mainly my purpose of visit, the subject of hypnotism and the occupations of the other dinner guests. It turned out that all our guests were on the payroll of the royal family. The occupations varied from teachers, gym fitness trainers, personal aids and yacht staff.

The Sultan owned a large yacht which was on permanent standby for his immediate boarding, if required. While anchored out at sea, the staff came ashore to relieve their boredom. An Australian girl who worked on board told me that the boat had not moved in six months and everybody was on full pay!

After a superb dinner and charming company, it was time to retire. The following day was going to be stressful enough and I was going to need all the rest I could get. Arrangements were made to have dinner again and, possibly, a party (with some smuggled alcohol) the next evening. As we requested the bill, everybody wanted to sign the cheque and a quarrel started as to who would. Crystal told me afterwards that everyone was on an unlimited expense account and it really didn't matter who signed.

The next morning I was up bright as a button. The weather in Brunei was superb and I managed to get in a little sunbathing at the pool. I noticed a party of girls gathering around, all dressed in official uniform. When they spotted me, they came over and asked for a group photograph. I agreed, but to this day I don't know why, as they certainly didn't know me or my purpose of visit. Crystal drove over to the hotel to take me back to the palace and on the way we discussed the running procedure for the show. Crystal was going to play the music for the show and then the bombshell was dropped – among the invited guests were the Sultan's wives, Her Majesty Raja Isteri Pengiran Anak Saleha and Her Royal Highness Pengiran Isteri Hajjah Mariam, and Princes Bahar and Hakim, Hamidah's brothers.

My pre-show nerves had now really set in. I was not allowed to hypnotise any of the royal family and the total of guests invited was forty. I knew I was going to have my work cut out. What made it worse was that several of the guests' grasp of the English language was not that good.

We did the necessary sound checks and then I found myself at a table where I waited for my call time. I needed to use the toilet and I asked a royal servant where the toilets where. She pointed them out – which all seemed fine until I got there – and out of the two available doors there were no markings to identify the boys' from the girls' so, despite being in a foreign place and surrounded with dignitaries – and on my very, very best behaviour – I crossed my fingers and took a chance, pushing hard on the right hand door.

As I burst in, I heard a loud, girly gasp of shock and surprise, catching a glimpse of a lady swathed in silks. I quickly backed out, bottom first, mumbling apologies, eyes tightly shut. I may even have bowed, I can't remember.

I had blundered unwittingly into the wrong toilet. I was so embarrassed. I walked back to my seat, holding my head in my hands, repeating, 'Gosh, what have I done!' Thankfully, it was not mentioned, they must have seen the funny side of my predicament.

Showtime was set for two in the afternoon; I was all set and most of the guests had arrived. Sound checks were completed and props were in place. The guests gathered around the stage area, lights went down and my intro set the atmosphere, 'Since the beginning of time, man has underestimated the power of the subconscious mind. Throughout human creation, certain people are born with special powers, and what you are about to see is live and unrehearsed. Allow yourself to relax, focus, and interact, for it is now time to welcome, live on stage, the true master of hypnosis, Mr Alan Bates.'

That was my cue. I made my entrance and my next words will stay with me for the rest of my life, it was a big point in my career.

'Your Royal Highnesses, Princess Pengearan Anak Hamidah, ladies and gentlemen, good afternoon!' I held the audience for the whole one-hour show, but I did struggle first of all in getting willing volunteers, and then when I did get six people on stage, three did not understand what I was saying and most of the audience did not know what I was doing. I ended up with three people hypnotised and, to my standards, I considered it a poor show. The royal family really did not have a clue what it was all about but I pulled it off and everybody was happy. I then retired to the dressing room, got changed and went off in search of a late lunch. I followed my nose to a massive lunch presentation 'fit for a king' – and queen, and a humble hypnotist!

I met up with Crystal and we had a debriefing on the show, ate lunch and discussed life in royal circles. Hamidah could have anything she wished for. She looked through designer catalogues and one of her seven nannies ordered everything in the catalogue. When the clothing arrived it was all in the wrong size. After apologising, the nanny offered to repack and send it back when Hamidah interrupted and said, 'Don't bother. Just reorder in my size.' Hamidah decided she wanted to learn how to dance so she hired a professional American dance team to stay in Brunei on a retainer so whenever her mood took her she would work out with the team.

Prince Jefri, I heard, was a real character and, I suppose, a real old-time playboy. He led an exorbitantly lavish lifestyle, until his assets were frozen and many of his possessions sold off. In fact, the media had reported he had probably gone through more cash than any other human being on earth. There were rumours that, at one point, he was spending $50 million a month. I was told many stories about him but I did not get to meet him and it was not my experience. I was invited as a guest of the royal family and they treated me very well, and we should speak as we actually find. I do not believe we should betray anyone's trust lightly.

When I returned to England I was offered a sum of several thousand pounds for my story by a journalist who wrote for a national daily tabloid. The money would have been nice but my moral compass would not allow me to tell. Since my visit to Brunei, many stories have leaked to the press about Prince Jefri's parties and activities, including a former Miss America beauty queen who started litigation in a US court claiming she had been invited over as a hostess but what was really wanted of her was sex.

I decided now my work was over it was time to have a tour of Prince Jefri's royal garage. Crystal took me down in her car and the only way I can explain it is – seeing is believing! The two garages ran side by side on two split-levels. Every model of Porsche lined the way, in every colour, followed by Ferrari in every colour, then on to Rolls Royce, Aston Martin, Mercedes, and every other make of prestige limited editions. Every vehicle was installed with a car phone and several mechanics were on duty to service and clean the machines. Apart from cars, there were top of the range motorbikes and tour buses with black glass windows. It was a fantastic experience alone just to see the garages and their contents.

Crystal suggested we go back to the palace and spend what little time we had left with Hamidah, as we were unsure if I would be invited back. Hamidah had a nice birthday. She was now fifteen and growing up quickly. We spent a further two hours walking and talking. She was inquisitive about life in England just as much as I was with life in Brunei.

It was time to say our goodbyes and in keeping with their tradition it is custom to give all guests a present. Rumours were going around that everybody was to receive a Rolex watch, but this was incorrect. Everybody queued up in turn to greet and wish the Princess a happy birthday and one of the royal aides on her behalf presented us all with a beautifully wrapped box.

When my turn came, I wished her again happy birthday and thanked her for my invitation. I also asked her if I could use, 'By Royal Appointment', on my stationary at home and she agreed.

Crystal and I made our way back to the car and, looking back over my shoulder as we left the royal grounds, I had to pinch myself to see if I had been dreaming. I was a very lucky man having experienced what I had. I was like a child at Christmas, opening my present. My gift? Well, that will remain my secret.

We made our way back to the hotel and Crystal arranged to meet our dinner guests from the previous night at 8.30 p.m. I managed to rest a while and take on board the day's events with a proud grin on my face. I made my way to the restaurant at our arranged time and I was informed that, after dinner, one of the guests had several bottles of vodka in his room and had invited everybody back. He also wanted me to hypnotise him. During dinner, a Ghurkha armed soldier came over to our table and requested a word with Crystal. We were concerned at what was happening when she came back to the table and said he had been instructed by Princess Hamidah to escort Mr Bates back to the royal palace as her Royal Highness wanted to see him! Crystal told him that I was feeling unwell and would not be able to go and he left. I will never know what she wanted that night, but after dinner we went to the party as arranged and enjoyed several vodkas. I also hypnotised two people at the party and gave everybody an entertaining time.

Once again, 'all good things must come to an end'. My time was up in Brunei and Crystal was going to take me back to the airport. I had just finished packing when I heard a knocking at my door. To my surprise, it was Princess Hamidah's bodyguard. I invited him in and he gave me an envelope. 'The Princess would like you to have this,' he explained. I thanked him and he left my room without a further word. I opened the large envelope and was delighted with its crisp sterling contents. The day was 27 April 1992. It was time for me to leave the kingdom and travel to my home kingdom, England.

The trip home was also an interesting experience. My connecting flight from Singapore to London gave me a six hour layover so I decided, along with a famous tennis champion that I met on the flight, to clear customs and head into the city. It was a wise decision. I found Singapore to be a fantastic place. We visited the famous Raffles Hotel, Orchard Road and several other attractions, and in no time we had to head back to the airport for our connection to London, unknown to me at the time that I would make lots of trips to Singapore in the future and perform at many venues, including the famous Tanglin Club, building a fan base, and make many good friends on the way.

It was now all over and I had one of the richest experiences one could ever wish to have.

Alan Bates, 'By Royal Appointment'.

Postscript

Several years later, while marketing my show in the UK, I received a letter from the Lord Chamberlain's Office at Buckingham Palace, in London, that read,

Dear Mr Bates,
I am in receipt of a letter, which you sent to the 'Event Organiser'. While it is kind of you to write and offer your services, I was a little surprised by the words 'by Royal Appointment' at the bottom of your writing paper as well on

your enclosed photograph. Certain companies who hold a Tradesman's Warrant for providing goods or services directly to a member of the Royal Family are permitted to use a similar form of words on their notepaper and certain other items. You do not hold such a warrant, and I therefore wonder by what authority you are using these words. I am afraid that unless you have documentary evidence to support this, you would have to remove these words from future material so that you do not mislead members of the public, who might otherwise think that you hold a Tradesman's Warrant.

Yours sincerely,

Jonathon Spencer.
Secretary Lord Chamberlain's Office.

I was fuming when I read the letter and promptly wrote back explaining my circumstances and connection with the Brunei Royal family. The very next day I received another letter from Buckingham Palace, from the secretary of the Lord Chamberlain's Office (as shown) that read as follows,

Dear Mr Bates,

Thank you for your letter dated the 25th October, and for explaining your connection with the Royal Family of Brunei. I am grateful to you for taking the trouble to do this, and for replying to my letter so promptly.

Signed yours sincerely,

Jonathon Spencer.
Secretary Lord Chamberlain's Office.

BUCKINGHAM PALACE

28th October, 1996

Dear Mr. Bates,

Thank you for your letter dated 25th October, and for explaining your connection with the Royal Family of Brunei.

I am grateful to you for taking the trouble to do this, and for replying to my letter so promptly.

Yours sincerely,

Jonathan Spencer
Secretary
Lord Chamberlain's Office

Alan Bates, Esq.,

This now brings me to the end of Confessions and I do hope that I have given you a giggle, and hopefully you have enjoyed the book.

Indeed, I have enjoyed writing it and in doing so it has brought back lots of fun memories of some crazy times from all over the world plus meetings with so many bizarre, lovely and outrageous people on the journey.

THE END

Made in the USA
Charleston, SC
19 April 2016